OVID: AMORES III

A Selection: 2, 4, 5, 14

OVID
AMORES III

A Selection: 2, 4, 5, 14

Edited by
Jennifer Ingleheart
and Katharine Radice

BLOOMSBURY

LONDON · NEW DELHI · NEW YORK · SYDNEY

Bloomsbury Academic

An imprint of Bloomsbury Publishing Plc

50 Bedford Square
London
WC1B 3DP
UK

1385 Broadway
New York
NY 10018
USA

www.bloomsbury.com

Bloomsbury is a registered trade mark of Bloomsbury Publishing Plc

First published in 2011 by Bristol Classical Press
Reprinted 2012
Reprinted by Bloomsbury Academic 2013

British Library Cataloguing-in-Publication Data
A catalogue record for this book is available from the British Library.

ISBN: PB: 978-1-8539-9745-7

Library of Congress Cataloging-in-Publication Data
A catalog record for this book is available from the Library of Congress.

Typeset by Ray Davies
Printed and bound in Great Britain

Contents

Preface

This book aims to help students in their study of the *Amores* 3 poems set for OCR AS level 2012-2014. We hope that given here is the material needed to facilitate and enrich that study, but not to limit or close down independent readings of the poems. We have included a comprehensive vocabulary list of words not included in the GCSE defined vocabulary list, language notes to help readers understand the more difficult patches of Latin, and a number of introductory essays. The General Introduction offers a brief account of the genre of love elegy, of Ovid, his poetry, and the *Amores* as a whole. In addition, each poem is accompanied by its own introduction: we hope that these will provide a starting point for the reader in building their own understanding. We have steered well clear of a line by line literary commentary, and we hope that the lack of this will encourage students to look at these poems with their own eyes.

Our thanks are due to Deborah Blake and her editorial team at Bloomsbury Academic, and to Stephen Anderson, who has given us the benefit of his meticulous attention to detail and his many years' experience of reading and teaching Latin.

Jennifer Ingleheart
Katharine Radice

General Introduction

This General Introduction briefly examines (i) Latin love elegy, (ii) Ovid in his contemporary context, and (iii) the characteristic features of his *Amores*; there is necessarily some overlap between these sections. Suggested further reading is provided at the end of each section.

Latin love elegy

Latin love elegy was already well established by the time Ovid's *Amores* were published under the principate of Augustus in the late first century BC. Catullus, who is usually believed to have lived from 84 to 54 BC, had written love poems (as well as verses on a variety of other themes) in the elegiac metre and provided an important model for later authors who treated erotic subjects, but love elegy itself is generally considered to have started with Gaius Cornelius Gallus. Born around 70 BC, Gallus is a shadowy figure who produced four books of elegies collectively entitled *Amores*, and who died in 27 or 26 BC. Very little survives of Gallus' work but he was obviously an important influence on Propertius and Tibullus – both born around 50 BC – as well as Ovid, the youngest of the major elegists. Ovid was born in 43 BC and began to recite his poetry in public as a teenager. These poems, about a beloved woman Ovid called Corinna, brought him instant fame, and were released in written form as the *Amores*, Ovid's first published collection and major contribution to Latin love elegy. The works of the Augustan elegists – Propertius, Tibullus and Ovid – have certain features in common, which enable us to talk about Latin love elegy as a 'genre', a type of poetry with recognisable shared elements; compare the modern film genres of the horror movie, say, or the romantic comedy, which give rise to certain expectations in their audiences. Each poet writing in the genre of Latin love elegy after Gallus would have been well aware that they were working in a tradition with established conventions, and this gives much scope for witty variation and innovation to authors – like Ovid – who were interested in playing with the rules of their chosen genre.

In the ancient world, poetry was distinguished from everyday speech by the fact that it was written in metre; ancient poetry was, after all, designed to be read aloud. Different genres of poetry used different metrical schemes; the metre of Latin love elegy was the elegiac couplet. These couplets always had as their first line a dactylic hexameter (the metre of the elevated epic genre), consisting of six feet, and named for one of its basic metrical units, the dactyl (– ◡ ◡). The dactyl is found in combination with the heavier spondee (– –) and hexameters can be scanned according to the following scheme:

$$ ^- \bar{\cup}\cup \mid ^- \bar{\cup}\cup \mid ^- \parallel \bar{\cup}\cup \mid ^- \bar{\cup}\cup \mid ^- \cup\cup \mid ^- \; ^- $$

Following the hexameter, came the shorter pentameter, a line of five feet, which is scanned as follows:

$$ ^- \bar{\cup}\cup \mid ^- \bar{\cup}\;\cup \mid ^- \parallel ^- \cup\cup \mid ^- \cup\;\cup \mid ^- $$

In addition to sharing a metre, Latin love elegies tend to treat the poet's overwhelming, devoted love for one woman, his *puella* ('girl') or *domina* ('mistress'). The latter term hints that the poet is enslaved to the woman he loves (a theme modern readers term the *servitium amoris* or 'slavery of love'), a shocking idea in ancient Rome, where slaves were property, bought and sold at their owners' whim, occupying the lowest position in society. As elegy's use of the metaphor of slavery suggests, elegiac love affairs tend to be far from happy; it is worth noting that in general English usage the word 'elegiac' can mean merely 'mournful' or 'pensive', whereas when used with reference to Latin poetry, it denotes the elegiac metre, which was itself believed to have originated in funeral laments and is therefore well suited to bemoaning the elegiac lover's circumstances.

There are numerous barriers to a blissful elegiac affair, including the cruel or unfaithful behaviour of the *domina*; the guard who chaperones the beloved and thus separates her from her lover; the figure of the rival lover; the *lena* (or 'madam'/ brothel-keeper) who encourages the *puella* to reject her devoted poet-lover in favour of a richer suitor. A significant further obstacle to the smooth course of an elegiac love affair comes from the beloved *puella*'s ongoing involvement in a relationship with another man, who may – or may not – be her husband, since the Latin word *vir* can mean 'husband', but alternatively, simply 'man' or 'boyfriend'. The potentially adulterous nature of elegiac relationships – to which we will return in the next section – is not the only way in which the elegists rejected the accepted standards of the society in which they lived: as we have already seen, the elegists shocked by presenting themselves as slaves to a woman, and they preferred the pursuit of love and leisure (or *otium*) to wealth or a serious career. Indeed, the elegists represent their love affairs as equivalent to waging war (a theme called the *militia amoris* or 'warfare of love'), an idea which was particularly provocative in the age of Augustus, where young men were expected to undergo military service as the boundaries of the Roman empire expanded. The elegists also revel in being *mollis* ('soft' or 'effeminate', a word they also use to characterise their love poetry) as opposed to *durus* ('hard', a characteristic they associate with those who hinder their love affairs or choose more conventional paths in life, such as soldiers or the epic poets who write about warfare and heroic deeds) as they reject public values for the different priorities of the private, elegiac world.

Further reading

On love elegy: Joan Booth, *Catullus to Ovid: Reading Latin Love Elegy* (London, 1995); R.O.A.M. Lyne, *The Latin Love Poets* (Oxford, 1980).

Translations of Latin love elegy: Guy Lee, *Ovid's Amores* (Oxford, 1961); A.D. Melville, *Ovid: The Love Poems* (Oxford, 1990).

Basic account of scansion of Latin hexameter and pentameter: B.H. Kennedy, *The Revised Latin Primer* (London, 1962), pp. 204-5.

Ovid and his poetry in context

Before we explore the place of the *Amores* in the elegiac tradition it is worth locating their author in his contemporary context. Publius Ovidius Naso provides us with most of the information which we possess about his life and poetic career in a later, autobiographical poem, *Tristia* 4.10. Ovid identifies the date of his birth (20 March, 43 BC), his birthplace (Sulmo, around one hundred miles from Rome), and his position as the second son of a family of established equestrian rank (a social status for which a minimum property qualification was required). Ovid's father was wealthy enough to send both of his sons to be educated in Rome, where they would have received the standard instruction of elite male Romans in Greek and Latin literature and in rhetoric (or the art of public speaking). Rhetorical education taught pupils how to argue a case persuasively and from a variety of different angles (the Introduction to 3.4 explains how Ovid does this in two paired poems) and to utilise mythical and historical examples to back up their case. Such training prepared young men for careers in the law courts or in public life. Ovid tells us that his older brother excelled as an orator before his untimely death at the age of twenty, and although other sources record that the youthful Ovid was also a promising public speaker (with a particular gift for the *suasoria*, or speech in which a certain course of action is advised: poems 4 and 14 in this collection are good examples of Ovid putting the *suasoria* to poetic use), Ovid himself claims that his only interest was in poetry from boyhood onwards – indeed, that whatever he tried to write came out as verse! His father, however, warned Ovid that even Homer made no money from poetry, and Ovid dutifully held a number of minor administrative and judicial posts, before rejecting a public career and devoting himself completely to a life of verse. Ovid's rhetorical training was not wasted, however, as he put to good use in his poetry the methods of legal argumentation and the ability to manipulate language that such education allowed him to hone; we shall see clear traces of the influence of Ovid's rhetorical training in our set texts (see further the Introductions to individual poems, in particular 3.4 and 3.14).

Ovid's use of words, however, led to his eventual downfall. *Tristia* 4.10, the source for most of the biographical information sketched above, was written in Tomi on the far-off shores of the Black Sea after Ovid was banished there in AD 8 by the emperor Augustus. The reasons for Ovid's exile have been much debated, but he himself gives two causes, *carmen et error* (*Tristia* 2.207), a 'poem and a mistake'. Ovid never fully reveals the nature of his mistake, but the poem can be identified as the *Ars amatoria* (or 'Art of Love'), which took the first-person situations and themes of Latin love elegy and turned them into a practical guide on seduction. The *Ars* thereby wittily developed a didactic strand already present in personal love elegy, as the elegists attempt to instruct a variety of audiences such as the inexperienced, first-time lover or the mistress herself, teaching her how to deceive her *uir*. Augustus, however, believed that the *Ars'* teaching was an incitement to wives to commit adultery and therefore banished its poet. The potentially adulterous nature of the relationships treated in elegy is relevant not only to Ovid's banishment but also to the understanding of many of the poems included in this volume, and therefore demands further consideration.

Adultery in the modern day tends to be viewed as a largely private matter, even though governments express concerns about the breakdown of marriages and families as the consequence of adulterous affairs. The situation was different in Rome. Marriages among elite Romans tended to be arranged rather than love matches. Moreover, standards were very different for men and women. Indulgence was traditionally granted to young Roman males who wished to pursue light-hearted love affairs with their social inferiors (such as freedwomen or prostitutes) before settling down and advancing their public careers through marriage alliances with influential and/or wealthy families. Roman wives, often many years their husband's junior, were, conversely, expected to be faithful to their husbands, providing them with legitimate heirs and thereby safeguarding the inheritance of property. It is perhaps hardly surprising, then, that adultery was widespread, despite limited private sanctions against it, such as the right of the wronged husband to return his wife to her family by divorcing her or even to kill adulterers caught *in flagrante delicto*.

In around 18 BC, however, adultery became a public concern, as the emperor Augustus introduced laws on marriage and adultery which encouraged all adult Roman citizens to enter into marriage and simultaneously made adultery a criminal offence subject to severe penalties. Augustus' motives for introducing such legislation are much debated – was it part of a personal crusade to reintroduce old-fashioned morality to a permissive society, an attempt to avert a recruitment crisis for the Roman army by keeping up the birthrate among citizens, a measure to ensure the smooth transition of property within the upper echelons of society, or a mixture of all of these? Whatever intentions lay behind the moral legislation, it aimed primarily at ensuring the fidelity of upper-class wives. One might object (as Ovid later did, to no avail) that Augustus' 18 BC legislation has little to do with the world of the elegists and vice versa: after all, love poetry in all genres had previously treated unambiguously adulterous relationships without being considered problematic. Besides, although Augustus' legislation attempted to enforce the fidelity of wives, different standards were in place for married men, who would be breaking the law if they had sex with another man's wife, but could still pursue some forms of extra-marital sex (for example, with prostitutes and slaves) with impunity. The social status of the elegiac *puella* is as unclear as the ambiguous vocabulary of the *vir*; she may be a respectable wife, but in most elegies it is equally possible that she is a prostitute and hence fair game sexually. Again, the elegists play with the possibility that the *puella* may be a fiction, a literary device which allows the elegists to treat the theme of love. Nevertheless, even fictional adultery was hardly a matter to be treated ambiguously or lightly after 18 BC.

The date of the Augustan moral legislation is important for the poems included in this volume: Ovid's *Amores* seem to have been composed from around 25 BC onwards, and cannot have been published later than 2 BC in their current form (an epigram at the start of the collection informs the reader that this is a shorter second edition, with five books slimmed down to the three that we now possess). All of the poems included in this volume are likely to post-date the moral legislation of 18 BC, and although it seems to have been the *didactic* nature of the *Ars* which particularly offended Augustus, offence may also have been caused by the lack of ambiguity in the portrayal of clearly adulterous relationships and the cheerful flouting of the spirit of the Augustan legislation in several of the poems in the *Amores* (see in particular the Introduction to 3.4).

Further reading

Andrew Wallace-Hadrill, *Augustan Rome* (Bristol, 1993) [useful background material on Augustus' principate, including the moral legislation].

Jennifer Ingleheart, 'Ovid's error: Actaeon, sex and striptease', *Omnibus* 52 (2006), 6-8 [on the mysterious error that led to Ovid's banishment].

Tristia 4.10: translation in A.D. Melville, *Ovid, Tristia: Sorrows of an Exile* (Oxford, 1992).

Ovid's *Amores*

The very title of the *Amores*, recalling that this is what Gallus had called his own elegiac collection, marks their debt to the genre. The opening couplet of the *Amores* likewise demonstrates Ovid's awareness of his literary heritage but also indicates that the *Amores*, despite their title, will not simply repeat the material found in earlier elegy. *Amores* 1.1 opens thus:

> Arma gravi numero violentaque bella parabam
> edere, materia conveniente modis.

> Arms and violent wars was I preparing to sing in a heavy metre,
> material fitted to its metre.

This is an intriguing opening to an elegiac collection on a number of levels. Love elegy traditionally treated the poet's overwhelming love for one woman: the first word of the first poem of Propertius' first collection had been 'Cynthia', the name of his mistress and the theme of many of his poems. Yet Ovid chooses to start his *Amores* with the word *Arma* ('arms' or 'weapons'), which had famously already been the opening word of

Virgil's great Augustan epic, the *Aeneid*, which promised to sing of the heroic theme of arms and the hero who wielded them. Hardly the subject matter that we expect from a love poet! Ovid's claims that he was preparing to write about warfare in the epic dactylic hexameter are equally unexpected. Here, after all, is a clearly elegiac couplet, with the epic hexameter followed by the shorter pentameter. As we read on, Ovid reveals why his second metrical foot is shorter than his first: the next couplet claims that Cupid, the mischievous god of love, stole away one foot, forcing Ovid to write in elegiac couplets rather than epic hexameters. It was traditional for ancient poets to say that they had been divinely inspired, but it was more usual to claim inspiration from Apollo or the Muses, gods with traditional responsibility for poetry; Ovid makes fun of the idea of divine poetic inspiration by treating his genre not as a serious mission given to him by Cupid but instead as the by-product of the playful boy-god's theft.

The opening four lines of *Amores* 1.1 therefore reveal much about Ovid's poetic manifesto or 'programme': he declares himself a literary joker, who teases readers with the possibility that he might write in a different genre and about topics which hardly suit love elegy, mocking the traditional poetic theme of divine inspiration. They also reveal that Ovid is concerned above all with poetry, rather than love: although we are not supposed to take seriously the idea that Ovid was composing an epic when Cupid intervened, Ovid's initial concentration on writing poetry rather than being in love is significant. It sets the scene for the rest of the collection, but more immediately for the remainder of this poem, in which Ovid first scolds Cupid for interfering with his poetry and then declares that he cannot be a love elegist because he is not in love: he does not have any subject matter suited to the genre, *aut puer aut longas compta puella comas* ('neither a boy nor a girl adorned with long hair', 20). Ovid here alludes to Tibullus' love elegies for a boy as well as the more traditional elegiac *puella*, teasingly suggesting that he might follow in Tibullus' footsteps (although in fact Ovid's personal love poems treat only love for women). However, an even bigger joke is that a love elegist, the poet of the *Amores*, does not have a beloved about whom he can write erotic poetry.

Cupid soon fixes this obstacle to Ovid's poetic career by shooting him with an arrow which causes him to fall in love. Ovid declares at lines 25-6:

> me miserum! certas habuit puer ille sagittas.
> uror, et in vacuo pectore regnat Amor.

> Wretched me! That boy had well-aimed arrows.
> I am on fire, and Cupid rules in my empty heart.

Ovid here simultaneously follows the rules of the elegiac genre and makes fun of them. His misery (*me miserum*, 25) is as conventional as the picture of the love poet burning with passion. But this is an odd sort of love poetry – how can Ovid be 'in love' and yet not be in love *with* someone specific? For Ovid never reveals the identity of the person he has fallen in love with in *Amores* 1.1, and the poem continues to focus on love poetry rather than love: Ovid concludes it by bidding farewell to epic battles and accepting the task of writing love elegy.

Ovid proceeds to further play with our expectations of the elegiac genre in the poems which follow. *Amores* 1.2 opens with a string of questions, as Ovid wonders why he is experiencing sleeplessness and disturbed nights before diagnosing his symptoms as those of love-sickness. Yet we still do not know *who* has caused Ovid's insomnia, and we might begin to question the sincerity of Ovid's suffering: it is, after all, strange that Ovid's first poem tells us that he has fallen in love but he seems unable to recognise the signs of passion at the start of the very next poem. This inconsistency highlights a gap between Ovid the poet and Ovid the lover: Ovid is detached from love, which appears more of a literary than a personal experience in his poetry. Ovid's disengagement from supposedly personal experiences is an important feature of the *Amores*; often Ovid the poet seems to be winking at his readers to let them know that this is a literary and erotic game rather than the record of a love affair. Ovid the poet places the character (or *persona*) of Ovid the lover in the situations typical of love elegy and invites the reader to smile at the lover's self-delusion, misery or lack of dignity. In other words, Ovid's knowing approach plays the pose of the anguished elegiac lover for laughs.

Such Ovidian game-playing is also on display in *Amores* 1.3, which finally reveals that Ovid is in love with an unnamed *puella*. Ovid declares his undying devotion and outlines his advantages as a boyfriend, including his ability to immortalise his beloved in verse: the final line claims *iunctaque semper erunt nomina nostra tuis* ('my name will always be joined with yours', 26). The reader may be forgiven for thinking this a romantic declaration, but the fact that Ovid's beloved still lacks a *name* might make us see this poem in a different light: since no named individual has yet been revealed as the 'one' to whom Ovid promises his eternal fidelity, such a claim could be used as a chat-up line on any woman who takes his fancy.

For, as we read Ovid's *Amores*, its title may turn out to be revealing: *amores*, the plural of the Latin word *amor* ('love'), can be used as a term of endearment for a single beloved, but alternatively it can have its full force as a plural noun, hinting at a string of love affairs. The earlier love elegists had sometimes failed to live up to their professed devotion to one woman – Tibullus, for example, has a boyfriend as well as a named mistress in his first book, then takes a new mistress in book 2. But Ovid barely bothers even to claim undying attachment to one woman. Ovid's beloved Corinna – who is finally named in the fifth poem when she turns up for an afternoon of sex with Ovid – is referred to by name in his poetry far less frequently than the mistresses of the earlier love elegists; we may assume that she is the unnamed mistress of at least some of the poems in which she is not named, although Ovid also has affairs with other named and unnamed women. Corinna is named only three times in the third book of the *Amores* and not in any of the poems which we will consider in this volume; she clearly cannot be identified with the *puella* in 3.2, where Ovid is trying to start a *new* love affair.

Love, then, is a light-hearted literary game in the *Amores*, as Ovid innovatively and wittily reworks traditional elegiac themes. What other features of these poems mark them out as distinctively Ovidian? I outline below a few of the most important aspects for the poems in this volume;

further comment can be found in the relevant introductory essays to each of our poems.

Poems in the *Amores* tend to be dramatic in nature: so, for example, of the poems in this collection, 3.2 presents us with a dramatic monologue set at the horse races; 3.4 and 3.14 are less clearly grounded in a particular location, but feature the poet's attempted persuasion (or *suasoria*) of an addressee; 3.5, which starts with an account of a dream, is revealed at lines 31-2 to be addressed to a dream-interpreter, whose interpretation is quoted as direct speech (although some have doubted that the poem is by Ovid; see further the Introduction to 3.5). Both Propertius and Tibullus had written dramatic poems, but their works tend to focus more on the inward contemplation of their feelings than the dramatic aspect of the situation in which they find themselves. Ovid exploits the dramatic potential of his poetry through small details which increase its immediacy, such as the use of exclamations, rhetorical questions, and the device of apostrophe (or direct address): for these features respectively, see e.g. 3.2.75, 39-40, and 7.

The dramatic aspect of the *Amores* is far from incompatible with their rhetorical nature. Ovid uses poems to explore a single theme comprehensively and ingeniously (so, for example, in contrast with earlier treatments of the theme of the *militia amoris*, which had made isolated connections between waging love and making war, *Amores* 1.9 explores, detail by detail, the myriad ways in which lovers are like soldiers; the same technique can be seen at work in the poems in our volume). Ovid also effectively pairs poems on the same theme but which make opposite cases (see the Introduction to 3.4), showing that he can turn his arguments to whatever cause he chooses. Furthermore, myth was frequently used in the rhetorical schools as a means of exemplifying arguments, and Ovid too employs mythical *exempla* extensively in his elegies, as had Propertius before him.

Above all, the *Amores* are notable for Ovid's mastery of both language and metre. Ovid's style is marked by verbal wit or wordplay which can manifest itself in numerous ways. One is the pointed repetition of the same phrase or word (or different grammatical forms of a word) as, for example, in 3.2.5; another is the way in which the word order echoes the sense, as at 3.4.24. Again, a common word can be used in an unusual way (see 3.4.5); compare 3.14.27, where the same verb governs two objects, one of which is expected and the other is decidedly not. This is poetry which strives to upset our expectations, to amusing effect (see 3.14.16). Ovid makes the elegiac couplet much more smooth and elegant than it is in the hands of, say, Propertius, and Ovid's control of his metre can be seen in the way in which he ensures balance and symmetry within couplets (which are essentially conceived of as self-contained units, with the pentameter often expanding or rephrasing the point of the hexameter) as well as within the two halves of each line. This can be illustrated with an example chosen at random from the poems in this volume (3.14.7-8):

> quis furor est, quae *nocte* latent, in *luce* fateri,
> et quae <u>clam</u> **facias facta** referre <u>palam</u>?

Words which are opposite in meaning (*nocte/ luce, clam/ palam*) balance each other within their line, with the contrast between the final pair of opposites enhanced by the fact of their rhyming. The pentameter revisits the hexameter's point, although in a more compressed, epigrammatic way, with greater use of repetition as two words which are different forms of the same verb (*facias* and *facta*) are placed next to each other, making Ovid's point about the paradoxical behaviour of his mistress succinctly and effectively. Compare too the way in which Ovid cleverly exploits the fast dactylic rhythm of the elegiac couplet in a poem which itself begins abruptly and is all about speed (see 3.2.1-2).

Further reading

Rebecca Armstrong, *Ovid and His Love Poetry* (London, 2005).

Amores 3.2

Introduction

Horse racing was an exciting and popular sport in ancient Rome; the famous racing scene from the 1959 film *Ben Hur*, which ends with the keyed-up crowd pouring into the arena at the race's conclusion, gives a fairly realistic flavour of the tense emotions involved. In *Amores* 3.2, addressed by Ovid to a fellow spectator, Ovid produces an equally dramatic account of a day at the races. This introductory essay analyses how Ovid vividly and impressionistically brings to life the experience of a Roman chariot race, from the sights and sounds to the dust which falls on the watching crowd. As we read the poem, it is almost as if we are listening over Ovid's shoulder as he talks to the woman sitting next to him. The poem therefore appears highly realistic but imagination also plays an important role: for much of this poem, as we shall see, Ovid lets his imagination run riot. This essay therefore explores this poem's blend of realism and fantasy, as Ovid brings horse racing and love together.

For Ovid's interest here, and in the *Amores*, is above all in love: the excitement of a day at the races for Ovid is *not* the thrill of the horses thundering past or backing a charioteer to win. Ovid has no interest in the horses, as he tells his neighbour right at the start of the poem: instead, he's come to watch *her* in the hope of beginning a love affair. Line 5 presents us with a scenario where the woman is watching the races, whereas Ovid is watching her (*tu cursus spectas, ego te*); the change in the case of the personal pronoun shows the woman first as the spectator of the races, then as the object of Ovid's gaze. Ovid goes on to point out that both he and the woman are spectators (*spectemus uterque*, 5) of what gives them pleasure (6), and the repetition of the verb *specto*, applied in the second instance in this line to both Ovid and his fellow spectator, highlights that they are very different kinds of spectators, one with a genuine interest in horse racing, the other focused on starting a love affair. Given that Ovid offers us a poem of seduction set at the races, this essay will also consider Ovid's seduction techniques.

The circus (or arena for horse racing) was an ideal place to start a new love affair, because here men and women could sit next to each other (3; 19-20), unlike in other venues such as the theatre or the gladiatorial amphitheatre. In the Roman world, marriages were usually arranged rather than love matches (see the General Introduction), and unmarried women and young wives were often shielded from male attention outside marriage. The separation of the sexes gives Latin love elegists some of their most characteristic complaints, as Ovid presents himself as the 'locked-out lover' singing a song outside his mistress' door or objects to the guard that a husband has set to watch over his wife (as in *Amores* 3.4). In the Roman circus, though, there were no such barriers to men and women mixing freely: here, Ovid can sit next to the woman and talk to her as he attempts to win her over, which he proceeds to do for the rest of our poem.

Ovid gives his readers the sense that they are present at the races through various techniques as the poem echoes the speed of the horses racing around the track in a number of ways. The first line's swift plunge into conversation is echoed by the metre as Ovid includes the maximum number of fast-moving dactyls possible in an elegiac couplet. The form of the poem therefore echoes the speed of events on the track, a speed which is maintained throughout the poem through the duplication of words, phrases and sounds, which gives the passage a swift, repetitive movement. A good example comes in line 11: *et modo lora dabo, modo vERbERe tERga notabo,* where several combinations of letters are repeated, as well as the word *modo*. Another example is when Ovid uses the same three word phrase (*invida vestis eras*) to start *and* end a couplet (27-8), giving it a wrap-around effect, rather like the way in which horses would circle the turning posts at either end of the arena and then start on a new lap of the same course. Ovid therefore uses the basic building blocks of the poem – its metre, the words chosen and their arrangement on the page – to reinforce a vivid picture of being at the races.

The realistic feel of the poem also stems from the way in which, although Ovid does not present us with a linear narrative of events, he nevertheless affords the reader an almost step-by-step account of the various stages of the races. The first 42 lines, focused on the experiences of the spectators, make the poem vivid by concentrating on what it must have been like to be present as a spectator, engaging the readers' senses in multiple ways. Ovid concentrates above all on the *sights* of the circus, from line 5 onwards, but does not neglect the sounds of the crowd, realistically evoked as Ovid follows his instruction to be quiet for the entrance of the procession of the gods (43) with the statement that *now* it's the time to applaud (44). Sight and sound are not the only senses to which Ovid appeals in this poem: the heat and the dust which affect the watching crowd also feature (37-40; 41-2) and such details help not only to build up a full picture of the experience of being a spectator, but also form a part of Ovid's seduction attempt (as we shall see). At line 43, however, Ovid suddenly switches his attention to the racing track, with the dramatic *sed iam pompa venit* marking the entrance of the procession of the gods which was customary before the races. At line 65, with another vivid marker of time (*iam*, 'now'), the praetor sets the horses off from their starting chambers. From this point up until line 82, it is almost as if Ovid is acting as a commentator on the action of the races: at line 67 he sees his neighbour's favourite charioteer, but he implies, rather than states, that this charioteer is making good progress by saying that the horses seem to know that she wants him to win (68). Just as the running order can switch from one second to the next in a race, so the situation in this poem often changes abruptly, and in the very next line, Ovid suddenly exclaims with disappointment that his charioteer has circled the turning post too wide. By taking the turning post tight, charioteers could gain a valuable time-advantage over their opponents, even though to do so could be risky. Ovid makes his implicit commentary on the progress of the race more lively at this point, by addressing the unfortunate charioteer himself (71), and asks his fellow spectators to demand a restart to the race, presenting this dramatically with a vivid *en* (75). Ovid appears more like a commentator than ever at lines 77-8 when he says, with another marker of time (*iam*), that now the starting gates are wide open again and that the horses are flying out from there. Again Ovid switches from commenting on what is happening on the track to heckling the charioteer that he is supporting when he encourages him (79). The race's speed is echoed in the speed of the movement of the poem's implied narrative at this point: after Ovid encourages the charioteer (79-80), the next thing we read is that Ovid's neighbour's prayers have come true (81) and that this charioteer has gained the palm that was awarded to victors (82). Ovid's focus, then, switches straight from the encouragement of the charioteer to the palm that marked his victory, leaving it to the reader's imagination to fill in the information that Ovid has left out. The sporting victory itself, the moment at which the successful charioteer crosses the winning line ahead of his competitors, is never actually recounted, fittingly enough for a poem which opens with Ovid's claim that he has no interest in the races. The poem therefore seems to give a real-time picture of events as they unfold, from the build-up to the race itself, and this makes it highly realistic.

Ovid, then, as we have seen, creates a realistic portrait of a day at the races through a variety of different techniques. As he tries to seduce his neighbour into becoming his latest mistress, though, he blends realism and fantasy in such a subtle manner that it can sometimes be hard to distinguish between them. This lends the poem much of its wit, as we shall see.

One case in which we can be sure that Ovid is merely fantasising occurs early on: at line 7, Ovid suddenly switches from addressing the girl herself to exclaiming how lucky her favourite charioteer is, which leads him on to develop a humorous fantasy of becoming a charioteer himself (9-14). Successful charioteers were major celebrities in ancient Rome and, just like top sportsmen nowadays, they must have attracted a certain following of women. The erotic implications of Ovid calling his neighbour's favourite charioteer lucky and then day-dreaming about becoming the charioteer are strengthened by similarities with an earlier *Amores* poem in which Ovid had fantasised about becoming something lucky enough to get close to his girlfriend: in *Amores* 2.15, Ovid imagines being transformed into his girlfriend's ring and accessing the parts of her that are hard for him to reach in his human form. If the idea of Ovid turning into a ring to get close to his mistress is ridiculous, the thought of a citizen and love poet like Ovid racing in the arena is equally improbable. Ovid flags up the lack of reality in this fantasy at lines 13-14 when he claims that he would drop his reins on the sight of his beloved. It would have been impossible for a Roman charioteer to do this, as the reins were wrapped around his body and had to be cut off in the event of an accident. Ovid therefore praises the woman sitting next to him by stressing the devastating effect of a single glance at her, while simultaneously demonstrating that, in his role as the pick-up artist of this poem, he does not know much about chariot racing; he really *is* here to seduce his neighbour rather than watch the horses. We can be sure that the poet Ovid knew that Roman charioteers could not drop their reins, but the ignorance of the figure of the lover in this poem wittily undermines Ovid's daydream of appearing as a charioteer, exposing it as merely a fantasy. But one thing that love elegists do know well is myth, and Ovid introduces the myth of Pelops at lines 15-18, claiming that on seeing his beloved Hippodamia, Pelops nearly lost the horse race he was competing in, but that her favour spurred him on to victory. The legendary King Oenomaus had received a prophecy that his son-in-law would kill him, and therefore challenged any suitors for his daughter Hippodamia to take part in a chariot race against him; if the suitors failed to win the race, they were executed. Ovid's use of this myth allows him to indulge in some outrageous flattery: myths in Latin love poetry are often used to compliment elegiac women by comparing them with famous beauties of legend, and Ovid's implication is that, in causing him to let go of his reins, the woman he is pursuing is even more good-looking and distracting than Hippodamia, for whom men were willing to risk their lives.

However, Ovid soon brings his audience back from the world of myth to contemporary reality: while Ovid has been plotting ways of getting closer to this woman, she may be keen to get away from him – line 19's direct question to her suggests that she may be moving as far away from him as she can. Rather than her next boyfriend, Ovid may represent an irritating distraction from the races for this woman. But Ovid's case is helped by the fact that, as he points out in lines 19-20, spectators were forced to sit next to each other in the circus. The fact that men and women are packed in together leads Ovid swiftly on (21-4) to warn the men sitting on her other side and behind her not to get too physically close to her. Ovid's warnings may be a chat-up technique, a way of presenting himself as concerned for the girl's welfare by protecting her from invasions of her personal space – a good tactic to make her think he'd be an attentive boyfriend. They may also be the product of Ovid's over-active imagination: Latin love elegy is full of rivals to the lover-poets, and Ovid's warnings to the man sitting on her other side and behind her may indicate that he suspects that he is not the only man who has come to the races in order to get closer to a woman. But Ovid may imagine the attentions of his 'rivals' – perhaps these men actually *have* come here to watch the races?

Ovid's imagination continues to be important as he next supposes that the girl's dress, which he notices trailing on the ground, is jealously covering up her legs so that nobody else can enjoy the sight of her (25-8). Just as Ovid had imagined in *Amores* 2.15 that a ring could feel physical desire for his mistress, so here he attributes a very human will – and his own desires – to the cloak. He compares this woman's legs with those of mythical women: Atalanta, the famous runner who was beaten by Milanion – sometimes better known as Hippomenes – in a celebrated footrace (about which Ovid later writes in *Metamorphoses* 10), and the goddess Diana, famous for hunting. Ovid's similes are simultaneously flattering and risqué: they compare his potential girlfriend with a goddess famed for her virginity, but also for the miniskirts that enabled her to be a successful huntress. Similarly, Atalanta would have had to wear a short tunic to run against men, whereas respectable Roman women wore dresses that went down as far as their feet. Given the images that the vision of this woman's legs sets off in Ovid's mind, it's not surprising that this glimpse inflames his passion further. Always prepared to let his imagination run riot, Ovid starts to fantasise about the parts of this woman that are concealed by her clothing. The normally very innocent and neutral phrase *et cetera* ('and the rest', 35) takes on a racy sense here as Ovid pictures the hidden charms of the woman sitting next to him.

When Ovid goes on to offer to fan this woman (37), at first glance this appears to be the sort of solicitous behaviour towards her that we have already seen in his warning to her neighbours not to invade her personal space. Yet Ovid soon reveals that his kind offer isn't in fact for her benefit. *He* is the one feeling the heat of the stadium (39), but Ovid turns this to his rhetorical advantage when he suggests that it might not be the heat of the air in the Circus that is having this effect, but rather the fires of passion that he feels for this woman (37-40). The idea that love is a flame or a fire is very common in ancient love poetry, but Ovid treats this clichéd metaphor *literally* here, wittily providing a neat compliment to his beloved by showing just how desirable she is, at the same time as he shows her that he knows how to speak the vocabulary of love.

The onward momentum of both the poem and of Ovid's seduction attempt is swift and seamless here as Ovid next worries about the dust that has fallen on his neighbour's dress and attempts to remove it (41-2). It is left to the reader to make the connection that the action of Ovid fanning his neighbour is what must have stirred up the dust in the first place. Removing the dust conveniently gives Ovid another opportunity to present himself as a devoted companion, the sort of boyfriend that a woman might want to sit next to her at the races, always ready to make sure that she does not suffer from the slightest discomfort. However, Ovid later revisits this first-person narrative of a day at the races in his *Ars amatoria* or *The Art of Love*, which presents many of the situations from the *Amores* as a practical guide on how to conduct affairs with members of the opposite sex. When Ovid reworks this scene in the *Ars*, he shows that seduction attempts need not be based on reality, advising men that they should brush away any dust which falls on the dress of the woman that they are interested in – even if there is no dust (*Ars* 1.149-52)!

Ovid is then distracted from removing dust from his neighbour by the procession of the statues of the gods (43). Fantasy plays an important role here, as Ovid claims that Venus has nodded consent to his prayer for erotic success (58). Gods were supposed to nod to show that they agreed to the favour that had been asked of them in the ancient world, but Ovid's claim cannot be taken seriously – Venus' nod here is after all that of a statue, an inanimate object that can hardly move its head! But this fantastic notion may perhaps have some basis in reality: the statue of the goddess might reasonably be expected to bob about as the procession progresses, and this, coupled with the distant view which spectators will have had of the procession, allows Ovid to interpret such movement as consent and thus to get away with such an outrageous claim and playful, witty conceit.

As the poem draws to a close, it becomes all but impossible to distinguish between reality and fantasy. In another rapid switch of attention from the action in the arena to the spectators, Ovid moves at line 82 from the charioteer's victory palm to thoughts that his own erotic victory is still to be won. The Latin love elegists more usually wish for military victory in their campaigns to win women, but here the traditional elegiac military triumph over the girl is replaced with visions of Ovid's sporting success; to gain the girl has become the equivalent of getting the victory palm, reminding us of Ovid's (ridiculous) earlier vision of himself as a successful charioteer. And, at first glance, success seems to be the note on which our poem ends – in the first line of the final couplet, Ovid moves away from addressing his neighbour to self-address. He notes that the woman has smiled, and that her eyes promise him *quiddam* ('something', 83); the final line of the poem then returns to directly addressing the woman, saying that this is enough, and demanding that she give him 'the rest' (*cetera*) in another location. We have already seen in this poem that the potentially very innocent word *cetera* can refer to the woman's hidden physical charms, and here too it lacks innocence, suggesting that sex will be the logical next step after the encouragement that this woman gives Ovid at the circus. Although Ovid presents himself as a masterly seducer of women in other poems, because so much of this poem seems to have been based on fantasy, the reader might question whether this woman's come-on is also taking place entirely within Ovid's head. After all, a woman whose favourite charioteer has just won a race might reasonably be expected to be smiling and to have shining eyes. The excitement of a day at the races – at least in terms of the love affair that Ovid tries to pursue at the circus – never reaches the fever-pitch in reality that it achieves in Ovid's over-active imagination.

Amores 3.2: Text

'Non ego nobilium sedeo studiosus equorum;
    cui tamen ipsa faves, vincat ut ille, precor.
ut loquerer tecum, veni, tecumque sederem,
    ne tibi non notus, quem facis, esset amor.
tu cursus spectas, ego te: spectemus uterque   5
    quod iuvat atque oculos pascat uterque suos.
o, cuicumque faves, felix agitator equorum!
    ergo illi curae contigit esse tuae?
hoc mihi contingat, sacro de carcere missis
    insistam forti mente vehendus equis   10
et modo lora dabo, modo verbere terga notabo,
    nunc stringam metas interiore rota;
si mihi currenti fueris conspecta, morabor,
    deque meis manibus lora remissa fluent.
a, quam paene Pelops Pisaea concidit hasta,   15
    dum spectat vultus, Hippodamia, tuos!
nempe favore suae vicit tamen ille puellae:
    vincamus dominae quisque favore suae.
quid frustra refugis? cogit nos linea iungi;
    haec in lege loci commoda Circus habet.   20
tu tamen, a dextra quicumque es, parce puellae:
    contactu lateris laeditur ista tui;
tu quoque, qui spectas post nos, tua contrahe crura,
    si pudor est, rigido nec preme terga genu.
sed nimium demissa iacent tibi pallia terra: 25
    collige, vel digitis en ego tollo meis.
invida vestis eras, quae tam bona crura tegebas;
    quoque magis spectes – invida vestis eras.

talia Milanion Atalantes crura fugacis
    optavit manibus sustinuisse suis;   30
talia pinguntur succinctae crura Dianae,
    cum sequitur fortes fortior ipsa feras.
his ego non visis arsi; quid fiet ab ipsis?
    in flammam flammas, in mare fundis aquas.
suspicor ex istis et cetera posse placere,   35
    quae bene sub tenui condita veste latent.
vis tamen interea faciles arcessere ventos,
    quos faciet nostra mota tabella manu?
an magis hic meus est animi, non aeris, aestus,
    captaque femineus pectora torret amor?   40
dum loquor, alba levi sparsa est tibi pulvere vestis:
    sordide de niveo corpore pulvis abi.
sed iam pompa venit: linguis animisque favete;
    tempus adest plausus: aurea pompa venit.
prima loco fertur passis Victoria pinnis: 45
    huc ades et meus hic fac, dea, vincat amor.
plaudite Neptuno, nimium qui creditis undis:
    nil mihi cum pelago; me mea terra capit.
plaude tuo Marti, miles: nos odimus arma;
    pax iuvat et media pace repertus amor.   50
auguribus Phoebus, Phoebe venantibus adsit;
    artifices in te verte, Minerva, manus.
ruricolae, Cereri teneroque assurgite Baccho;
    Pollucem pugiles, Castora placet eques.
nos tibi, blanda Venus, puerisque potentibus arcu   55
    plaudimus: inceptis adnue, diva, meis
daque novae mentem dominae, patiatur amari;
    adnuit et motu signa secunda dedit.
quod dea promisit, promittas ipsa rogamus:
    pace loquar Veneris, tu dea maior eris.   60
per tibi tot iuro testes pompamque deorum
    te dominam nobis tempus in omne peti.

sed pendent tibi crura: potes, si forte iuvabit,
    cancellis primos inseruisse pedes.
maxima iam vacuo praetor spectacula Circo   65
    quadriiugos aequo carcere misit equos.
cui studeas, video; vincet, cuicumque favebis:
    quid cupias, ipsi scire videntur equi.
me miserum! metam spatioso circumit orbe;
    quid facis? admoto proximus axe subit.   70
quid facis, infelix? perdis bona vota puellae;
    tende, precor, valida lora sinistra manu.
favimus ignavo. sed enim revocate, Quirites,
    et date iactatis undique signa togis.
en revocant; at, ne turbet toga mota capillos,   75
    in nostros abdas te licet usque sinus.
iamque patent iterum reserato carcere postes,
    evolat admissis discolor agmen equis.
nunc saltem supera spatioque insurge patenti:
    sint mea, sint dominae fac rata vota meae.   80
sunt dominae rata vota meae, mea vota supersunt;
    ille tenet palmam, palma petenda mea est.'
risit et argutis quiddam promisit ocellis:
    'hoc satis est; alio cetera redde loco.'

Amores 3.2: Notes

Line 1: *studiosus* is followed here by an objective genitive (*nobilium ... equorum*), so called because the noun plays the role of object to the idea of the action contained in the adjective *studiosus*. *nobilium* – 'thoroughbred'.

Line 2: *ille* is the antecedent for *cui*; *vincat ut ille* is the indirect command following upon *precor* (translate as *ut ille vincat*).

Line 4: notice that the double negatives cancel each other out, as in English ('so that the love ... might not be unknown ...'); *amor* is the antecedent to the relative *quem*.

Line 5: *spectemus*: jussive subjunctive – 'let us watch'.

Line 8: *contigit* – used impersonally here (+ dative + infinitive). *curae ... tuae* – predicative dative, working with *esse*: 'to be (as) your concern'; the possessive adjective *tuae* is Ovid's variation on the much more common *curae esse tibi* ('to be (as) a concern to you').

Line 9: *contingat*: subjunctive used to express a wish – 'may it befall ...'. *sacro de carcere*: the starting-box (*carcer*) is described here as sacred probably as a general reference to the religious festival of which the games were a part, but it is possibly a more specific reference to the statues of gods which some think were on top of the *carceres*.

Line 10: *insistam:* future indicative; *vehendus* – the gerundive here works in place of the non-existent passive present participle – the passive of *veho* gives a sense of 'I am carried' and so (if by horse) 'I ride': translate therefore as 'riding'.

Line 13: *fueris conspecta* is broadly equivalent to the future perfect form *conspecta eris*, but *fueris* increases the sense of completion of the action, and so the sense that the action happens in a split second (the idea is that Ovid will catch a glimpse as he speeds by); notice, however, that the future perfect in a conditional clause is translated into the English present tense – 'if you are seen ...'. *mihi currenti* – dative here, rather than *a(b)* + ablative, probably containing the sense of a dative of advantage: it is not just that she might be seen by him, but that the sight will matter to Ovid.

Line 15: *a* – marks an exclamation (cf. English 'oh'). Pelops was a great and ancient mythological Greek hero (grandfather to Agamemnon who was the most powerful Greek king at the time of the Trojan war). Poseidon gave to Pelops a golden chariot and a team of immortal horses; using these, in order to win Hippodamia's hand in marriage, he competed in a chariot race against her father Oenomaus, king of Pisa and Elis. This chariot race is shown on the East pediment of the temple to Zeus at Olympia. For a discussion of Ovid's use of myth, see the introduction to this poem. *Pisaea ... hasta* – 'the spear of Oenomaus'.

Line 16: *dum spectat* – *dum* is always followed by the present indicative when it means 'at some point during' (distinguish between this and when *while* means 'all the time that'), but translate here into a past tense in English.

Line 18: *vincamus*: jussive subjunctive.

Line 19: *quid* – translate here as 'why?'. *cogit nos linea habet*: lines were drawn on the stone benches to mark out the seats, and each spectator was supposed to sit within the space allocated.

Line 20: *in lege loci*: 'in its rule for seating'.

Line 21: *a dextra:* 'on the right'.

Line 22: *contactu lateris ... tui*: since the genitive is generally used in Latin when one noun follows upon another, its meaning covers a far greater span than the English 'of', and so here: 'contact with ...'.

Line 24: *nec* contains the conjunction to join the two imperatives *contrahe* and *preme*, and so translate before *si*.

Line 25: *nimium demissa*: 'slipping down too far'. *tibi* – essentially a possessive dative (and so equivalent to 'your'), but the dative allows for a sense of disadvantage, i.e. that the girl should mind that her cloak is on the ground. *terra* – the ablative used here to show position ('on the ground').

Line 26: *vel* – gives the alternative to *collige* ('Gather it up – or – look! – I am lifting it ...').

Line 28: *quŏque* not *quoque*. The meaning of *quoque magis spectes* is 'and the more one looks', but the *eo magis ...* ('the more ...') needed to complete the sense has been replaced by the exclamation *invida vestis eras*. Ovid's change in construction implies that as he looks at her legs he breaks off mid sentence to exclaim 'you *were* an envious garment'.

Line 29: *Atalantes* – a transliteration of the Greek genitive form. Atalanta was famous for both her speed in running and her chastity: she made her suitors compete against her in a running race, and was eventually beaten by Milanion (Hippomenes in Ovid's own version of the myth – see *Metamorphoses* 10).

Line 30: *sustinuisse* – the perfect tense gives a sense of completion, but this is hard to capture in English, so probably best to translate as a present infinitive: 'he wished to hold ...'.

Line 31: Diana – the goddess of hunting (and chastity) – is often painted with her dress tucked up into her belt so that she could run more quickly.

For a discussion of Ovid's use of similes here, see the introduction to this poem.

Line 32: *cum* takes the indicative when it has no sense of 'since' and means only 'when'.

Lines 35-6: *et* – 'also', 'too'; *cetera* is the antecedent to *quae;* translate *bene* with *condita*.

Line 37: *faciles* – here 'soft / gentle'.

Line 38: *tabella* – usually a small writing tablet, but probably here means the girl's fan. *nostra* (ablative) in agreement with *manu*.

Line 39: *an* introduces a second question, often following upon a previous question containing a sense of doubt: *an magis hic meus est animi, non aeris aestus* – 'or is this heat instead mine, of my heart, not of the air?' (in better English: 'or is this the heat of my heart, not of the air?').

Line 41: *dum loquor* – see note on line 16; *tibi* – see note on line 25.

Line 42: *sordide ... pulvis* – vocative.

Line 43: *pompa* – statues of the gods were carried out in procession immediately before the start of the races. *linguis animisque favete* – 'show support with voice and mind', i.e. keep quiet and pay attention (a standard invocation for the start of a religious ceremony).

Line 44: *tempus ... plausus* – *plausus* is genitive, so 'time for applause' – see note on line 22.

Line 45: *prima* agrees with *Victoria,* so in English 'First in position Victory is carried ...'. *passis ... pinnis* – 'with wings spread out'.

Line 46: *ades* – imperative of *adsum*, but combined with *huc* ('hither') gives a sense of 'come here'. *fac ut* + present subjunctive means 'see to it that ...', but the *ut* can be omitted, as here: translate as *fac (ut) hic meus amor vincat. hic* here is the pronoun used adjectivally, not the adverb, so 'this love of mine'.

Line 47: *Neptuno* – dative as the indirect object of *plaudite* ('give applause for Neptune') – see also lines 49 and 55-6. *qui* has as its antecedent those addressed by the imperative ('O you who ...').

Line 48: *nil mihi cum pelago* – 'the sea is no concern of mine'.

Line 51: *adsit* – subjunctive used to express a wish; *adsum* often has the sense of 'be favourable to' when used of deities, so here: 'May Phoebus be favourable to his augurs, may Phoebe be favourable to her hunters'. Augurs were Rome's official diviners, appointed to interpret signs sent from the gods, most often through birds, thunder and lightning. Phoebe is another name for the goddess Diana, sister of Phoebus (Apollo). Diana was associated particularly with hunting, Apollo with prophecy.

Line 52: *artifices ... manus* – 'the craftsmen's hands': Ovid is inviting Minerva (goddess of wisdom, science and creative arts) to direct to herself applause from her supporters.

Line 53: Ceres (god of agriculture) and Bacchus (god of wine and the vine) were the protective deities of the farmers. *tenero* is used here to describe Bacchus, but invites us to think of the vines he watches over because it is more obviously applicable thus.

Line 54: *placet* – jussive subjunctive from *placo -are,* which here has the meaning 'win the favour of'. Both *pugiles* and *eques* are the subjects of *placet*, which is singular by attraction to its closer subject (*eques*). *eques* is a poetic singular for plural (cf. *nos* in line 55 where the plural is used instead of the singular *ego*); convention allowed poets this flexibility as a way to write more easily within the strict metre. Castor and Pollux were the twin brothers of Helen of Troy and were famous mythological heroes (sailing on board the Argo with Jason, for example) who were subsequently deified. Pollux was renowned for his skill at boxing, but both were particularly famous horseman, and according to Roman legend, had appeared on earth to support the Romans in their fight against the Latins in the battle of Lake Regillus in 484 BC. Thereafter, they became part of Roman cult, worshipped especially by the *equites*.

Line 55: *puerisque potentibus arcu*: a reference to Cupid and the other love-sprites, the deities who made mortals fall in love. Their bows and arrows are symbolic of both love's power, and the often unwitting nature of their targets.

Line 57: *mentem* – here: 'right mind'; *novae ... dominae* – Ovid's 'new mistress' implies that he is in love not for the first time. *patiatur* – the *ut* is omitted (literally 'give my new mistress the right mind to allow herself to be loved').

Line 58: *motu* refers to the nod of the head conveyed by *adnuit*. Ovid imagines that he has seen the statue of Venus nod assent. The blending of reality and imagination is an important part of this poem and is discussed in the introduction.

Line 59: Translate as *rogamus (ut) ipsa promittas (id) quod dea promisit.*

Line 60: *pace ... Veneris*: 'with the grace of Venus': Ovid needs to appeal to Venus' indulgence to make the bold claim *tu dea maior eris.*

Lines 61-2: In oaths, *per* (+ acc) – 'by ...'. *tibi ... iuro ... te dominam nobis ... peti*: accusative + infinitive following *iuro* – 'I swear to you ... that you are sought as my mistress ...'. Notice *in* with the accusative here: 'for all time'.

Line 63: *tibi* – possessive dative.

Line 64: *primos ... pedes*: 'the tips of your toes'. *inseruisse*: the perfect infinitive gives a sense of completed action: the meaning is not so much that the girl can go through the process of inserting her toes into the grating, but that she can sit with them in there (cf. line 30).

Lines 65-6: *praetor* – the praetors were among Rome's most senior magistrates, second in rank to the consuls. Their remit included overseeing the legal system and big public events such as the games. *vacuo ... Circo* – an ablative absolute with the (non-existent) present participle of *sum* understood: 'the circus now being clear'. *maxima ... spectacula* and *quadriiugos ... equos* are in apposition to each other: 'the praetor has released the four-horse teams, the greatest show ...'. *aequo carcere* – the starting gates were not level as *aequo* might imply, but staggered in order to equalise the distance from the turning point and make it a fair race.

Line 67: *cui studeas, video*: the subjunctive *studeas* shows that *cui* is the interrogative pronoun, not the relative, and so introduces an indirect question: 'I see who you are supporting'.

Line 68: Translate as *equi ipsi videntur scire quid cupias*.

Line 69: *me miserum*: accusative used here for an exclamation (as in English): 'oh, wretched me!' *metam*: the turning points at either end of the racecourse were notoriously difficult – charioteers would aim to turn as tightly as possible in order to minimise distance and maximise speed, but too tight a turn could lead to instant defeat (even death) as their horses collided and chariots overturned.

Line 70: *admoto .... axe* (lit: 'his wheel brought close') may well be in contrast to *spatioso ... orbe*; if so then the sense is 'the nearest driver, *having steered a tight turn*, is right upon you'.

Line 72: Scansion shows *validā*, so the adjective agrees with *manu*, and *sinistra* with *lora*.

Line 73: *sed enim* – 'but indeed'.

Lines 73-4: The copious folds of a toga had to be held up by the wearer bending his left arm; by flinging these down, the spectators could demand a fresh start to the race.

Line 75: *mota* – Latin does not have an intransitive verb for *move*, and so has to use the perfect passive participle here to capture the sense of 'moving'.

Line 76: *licet ut* + present subjunctive – 'it is allowed that ...' ; as with *fac* (see note on line 46) the *ut* can be omitted, so *licet abdas te* – 'you can hide yourself'.

Line 78: *discolor*: the charioteers wore different colours so that they could be easily identified.

Line 79: *spatioque insurge patenti* – '... and press ahead in the open space'.

Line 80: Translate as *fac (ut) vota mea sint rata, vota dominae meae sint rata* (see note on line 46).

Line 82: A palm-frond was the medal given to the winner of the race.

Line 83: *quiddam* not *quoddam* because used here as a noun, not an adjective. *ocellus* is the diminutive form of *oculus*.

Line 84: A very suggestive final line: 'That's enough; give me the rest elsewhere!'

Amores 3.4

Introduction

A light-heartedly immoral poem on a serious subject. Ovid addresses a *Dure vir* ('Harsh husband', 1) who plays the role expected of such a figure in elegy by obstructing the love affairs of his wife, contrasted with her strict spouse as a *tener ... puella* ('a tender girl', 1). Ovid attempts to persuade the husband that his efforts to guard his wife and so ensure her fidelity are in vain. The major attraction of this poem is Ovid's rhetorical brilliance and wit as he revisits earlier elegies on similar topics, including one of his own previous *Amores* poems. Ovid's rhetoric here unapologetically promotes adultery, making the poem outrageously provocative in its contemporary context (for more on elegy and adultery, see General Introduction). This essay therefore examines how *Amores* 3.4 develops its models, and the ways in which Ovid's rhetorical skills are deployed, before considering the poem's potential to cause offence in its contemporary context; there is necessarily some overlap between these areas in Ovid's tightly argued *suasoria* (for this term, see General Introduction).

The *custos* ('guard', 1) intended to ensure the fidelity of a *puella* is a familiar elegiac figure from poems such as *Amores* 2.2, in which Ovid tries to persuade a guard to watch over Ovid's *puella* less carefully. In *Amores* 3.4, the poet's powers of persuasion are aimed not at the *custos* himself but instead at the *vir* who keeps his wife under surveillance. The earlier *Amores* 2.19 (provided in translation on pp. 79-80 of this volume) had advised a *vir* to ensure that his *puella* is closely guarded, because Ovid wants a *custos* to add spice to his affair with her: *Amores* 2.19 claims that passion is increased by obstacles, outrageously asserting that the barriers which usually cause anguish to the poet are an aspect of the elegiac love affair Ovid positively relishes. Our poem is therefore clearly paired with

41

and reworks *Amores* 2.19, undoing Ovid's earlier advice to guard a *puella* carefully. It is never directly stated in our poem that Ovid is encouraging the husband to guard his wife less carefully in order to facilitate *Ovid*'s own affair with her. However, close links with *Amores* 2.19 make it reasonable to infer that Ovid's earlier advice to the husband to guard his wife has been all too successful, and that Ovid is now asking the same husband to relax his vigilance for his own benefit. Taken together with 2.19, our poem provides an excellent example of Ovid turning his rhetorical education to poetic advantage. For these poems approach the same basic situation, yet try to persuade the *vir* to opposite courses of action; taken together, they demonstrate Ovid's ability to turn his arguments to fit any case, deploying many of the same rhetorical techniques and skills (for Ovid's rhetorical training, which taught orators to argue the same issue from different standpoints, see the General Introduction).

Both *Amores* 2.19 and this poem introduce arguments that initially surprise; it is, after all, more usual for an elegist to complain at being forcibly separated from his mistress than urge her husband to guard her carefully, as happens in 2.19. Our poem also surprises expectations by opening in a moralistic manner, claiming that chastity is innate, and cannot be imposed (1-8). The notion that a woman sins through her thoughts rather than her deeds (4), which leads Ovid to label the mind *adultera* (5; a strikingly original image: *adultera* was normally used as a noun rather than an adjective), is comparable to Christian ideas about sin and intention. The rhetoric convinces because the reader is fooled by the apparently serious opening and the progression of Ovid's arguments throughout the poem. Putting moralistic arguments to an immoral end makes them humorous, and the outrageous wit of Ovid's rhetoric increases as the poem moves on to claims that ease of access removes temptation (9-18), followed by the assertion that guards are in any case useless (19-24). Ovid then moves to a bolder argument: that guards actually encourage adultery (25-36), since what is forbidden is attractive. The poem then culminates in the most outrageously immoral assertion of all: that the husband should permit his wife to act as she pleases, and benefit from the gifts that his rivals will bring to him (see further below).

In order to advance these various strands of his argument, Ovid uses a range of different rhetorical techniques, demonstrating his skill and ability to marshal varied material in support of his case. The analogy of the horse (13-16), introduced from Ovid's own experience (*vidi ego*, 13, makes this hackneyed general illustration seem more personal), recalls the frequent use of examples from nature in Roman oratory. It was also usual in Roman oratory to use examples from myth or history to back up a case, as Ovid does here at lines 19-24 and 39-40 respectively (see further below for a discussion of how these examples are deployed). In Roman law courts, orators would address direct questions to those present, as Ovid does here at (e.g.) 35-6 and 41. Such direct (yet rhetorical – Ovid does not expect an answer) questions increase the dramatic texture of the poem, making it seem like a genuine attempt to persuade the husband. In fact, the poem is rather a virtuoso exercise in rhetorical skill.

Ovid's rhetorical skills are very much on display in his use of mythological *exempla* (or examples) at lines 19-24. Ovid's use of myth is anticipated in line 18's reference to the sick man who hankers after water, which will have reminded ancient readers of the myth of Tantalus, eternally punished in the Underworld by being unable to drink from the pool of water in which he was standing (hence the modern verb 'tantalise'). Then, in order to illustrate Ovid's claim that humans hanker after the forbidden, lines 19-22 pair two myths (those of Io and Danaë, both of whom were subject to close surveillance) which Ovid had already used in combination to make the same point at *Amores* 2.19.27-30. Ovid, however, varies his use of these myths. So, for example, in 2.19, Danaë is found before Io, an order reversed here, and the recycling of these myths means that Io does not need to be named here, whereas she had been at 2.19.29. More importantly, in 3.4 these myths bolster Ovid's additional point that erotic obstacles are futile, which is underlined by Ovid's emphasis on the two hundred eyes (*centum ... centum*, 19) of the *custos* Argus nevertheless being fooled by the single (*unus*, 20) personified Amor or Cupid. Nowhere else does Argus have so many eyes; the exaggeration in contrast with the single *Amor* reinforces Ovid's point well. Ovid then unexpectedly adds a third myth to the pair found in 2.19: Penelope's devotion, despite the lack of a guard, to her husband Odysseus (23-4). This was a very famous myth: Homer's *Odyssey* depicts Penelope's fidelity during the many years while her husband, Odysseus, was away in Troy and trying to make his way home; the story's fame means that Ovid need not name Penelope's husband. The proverbially chaste Penelope who lacked a guard provides an obvious contrast to the unchaste, yet well guarded Io and Danaë. Yet Ovid's reference to this myth might trouble any husband: although Ovid emphasises that Penelope remained a byword for wifely devotion, she is nevertheless surrounded by suitors (literally, with *iuvenes ... procos* wittily enclosing the *intemerata* Penelope in line 24). Ovid's emphasis on the multitude of Penelope's suitors (*tot*, 24), *quamvis custode carebat* ('although she was lacking a guard', 23), slyly undermines the immediately following claim that whatever is guarded is more greatly desired (25). The use of the myth of Penelope as a paragon of wifely virtue straight after two examples of mythical 'loose women' also hints that Penelope is the exception rather than the rule.

The *adulterous* aspect of the basic scenario is another important element which our poem draws on and develops from *Amores* 2.19. The term *vir* is frequently exploited for its ambiguity in elegy (see General Introduction), but the reader of 2.19 is left in no doubt that adultery is involved when Ovid brands the man who fails to provide obstacles to Ovid's affair with his wife a *leno maritus* ('a husband who is a pimp', 57). Similarly, the vocabulary of our poem repeatedly emphasises adultery: in addition to *adultera mens* (5), *adulter* (8), *adultera* (29), *adultera coniunx* (37), the terms *uxor* (45) and *maritus* (27) clearly indicate the legal status of the *vir* and his *puella*. The potential offence caused by the adulterous aspect of these poems is increased in *Amores* 3.4 by the fact that adultery is not the only criminal act which Ovid encourages. Augustus' 18 BC moral legislation had also introduced the new offence of *lenocinium* (a term defined by the legal textbooks as the keeping of female prostitutes for profit, or 'pimping'), which meant that wronged husbands who failed to divorce their adulterous wives and expose them to the penalties of the

Augustan law were treated as accessories to the adultery. Overlooking a wife's misbehaviour was seen as pimping because husbands apparently often benefited materially from their wives' affairs, as her lovers offered gifts as incentives to turn a blind eye. When Ovid brands the husband of *Amores* 2.19 a *leno maritus*, the term is metaphorical, commenting merely on the husband's failure to obstruct Ovid's affair, but in *Amores* 3.4 the theme is outrageously literal, as Ovid raises the stakes by advising the husband of this poem to take advantage of his wife's infidelity by accepting her lovers' gifts (45-8); this is a staggeringly immoral position, not least because the inheritance of property by legitimate heirs was a major reason for disapproval of adultery (see further the General Introduction). Ovid cannot have been unaware of the potential for thus offending Augustus, not least because the publication of a second edition of the *Amores* (the collection which we now possess: see General Introduction) must have come after the 18 BC legislation.

The provocation that our poem offers to the Augustan regime by encouraging courses of action forbidden by law is paralleled elsewhere in 3.4. At lines 37-8, Ovid claims that the husband who objects to his wife's adulteries is *rusticus ... nimium* ('too rustic') and not well enough acquainted with the sophisticated ways of Rome. The contrast between countryside and city is a staple of Augustan literature and thought, where the countryside is traditionally equated with morality and old-fashioned Italian values, a notion in line with the Augustan regime's emphasis on 'back to basics' morality. However, for those of a different tendency, such as Ovid, rusticity is a sign of stick-in-the-mud, laughably outdated tendencies. The next couplet (39-40) caps the affront to Augustan ideals, as Ovid links the city of Rome with sexual immorality by reference to its foundation myth. He alludes to the fact that the twins Romulus (the city's founder) and Remus were born to the Trojan princess Ilia as a result of her rape by Mars, the god of war. Ovid does not refer directly to the rape, preferring to talk around it with the periphrasis *non sunt sine crimine nati* ('they were not born without guilt', 39). The couplet is elevated in tone, with the compound adjective *Martigenae* ('born of Mars', 39) suggesting the origin of Roman military supremacy, and the pentameter consisting entirely of proper names (40) sounds very grand as Ovid refers to both twins with the epic matronymic *Iliades* ('son of Ilia'; it is more usual for patronymics, naming the father, to be used in epic). The high-sounding language is, however, undermined by its context, as the sons of Ilia are used to illustrate that sexual immorality was an innate Roman quality from the city's very foundation. Augustus was keen to emphasise both the descent of the Romans from their Trojan ancestors and the role of Romulus as founder of the city, which anticipated his own self-presentation as the second founder of Rome after the civil wars. However, Ovid's emphasis on sexual irregularity as part of the heritage of the Romans is something that Augustan propaganda was understandably less keen to emphasise. The breathtaking outrageousness of such engagement with the ideas of Augustus is only outdone by the poem's concluding advice to the husband to behave as a *leno* (on which, see further above). This poem therefore goes further than perhaps any other single elegy in the *Amores* collection towards providing offence to the Augustan regime.

Amores 3.4: Text

Dure vir, inposito tenerae custode puellae
    nil agis: ingenio est quaeque tuenda suo.
si qua metu dempto casta est, ea denique casta est;
    quae, quia non liceat, non facit, illa facit.
ut iam servaris bene corpus, adultera mens est   5
    nec custodiri, ne velit, ulla potest;
nec corpus servare potes, licet omnia claudas:
    omnibus occlusis intus adulter erit.
cui peccare licet, peccat minus: ipsa potestas
    semina nequitiae languidiora facit.   10
desine, crede mihi, vitia inritare vetando;
    obsequio vinces aptius illa tuo.
vidi ego nuper equum contra sua vincla tenacem
    ore reluctanti fulminis ire modo;
constitit, ut primum concessas sensit habenas   15
    frenaque in effusa laxa iacere iuba.
nitimur in vetitum semper cupimusque negata:
    sic interdictis imminet aeger aquis.
centum fronte oculos, centum cervice gerebat
    Argus, et hos unus saepe fefellit Amor;   20
in thalamum Danae ferro saxoque perennem
    quae fuerat virgo tradita, mater erat:
Penelope mansit, quamvis custode carebat,
    inter tot iuvenes intemerata procos.
quidquid servatur, cupimus magis, ipsaque furem   25
    cura vocat; pauci, quod sinit alter, amant.
nec facie placet illa sua, sed amore mariti:
    nescioquid, quod te ceperit, esse putant.

non proba fit, quam vir servat, sed adultera cara:
　　ipse timor pretium corpore maius habet.　　　　　　　30
indignere licet, iuvat inconcessa voluptas:
　　sola placet, 'timeo' dicere si qua potest.
nec tamen ingenuam ius est servare puellam;
　　hic metus externae corpora gentis agat.
scilicet ut possit custos 'ego' dicere 'feci',　　　　　　35
　　in laudem servi casta sit illa tui?
rusticus est nimium, quem laedit adultera coniunx,
　　et notos mores non satis Urbis habet,
in qua Martigenae non sunt sine crimine nati
　　Romulus Iliades Iliadesque Remus.　　　　　　　40
quo tibi formosam, si non nisi casta placebat?
　　non possunt ullis ista coire modis.
si sapis, indulge dominae vultusque severos
　　exue nec rigidi iura tuere viri
et cole quos dederit (multos dabit) uxor amicos:　　　　45
　　gratia sic minimo magna labore venit;
sic poteris iuvenum convivia semper inire
　　et, quae non dederis, multa videre domi.

Amores 3.4: Notes

Line 1: *Dure vir* – vocative; Ovid is addressing a husband who is overly zealous in guarding his wife's fidelity.

Line 2: *nil agis* – 'you achieve nothing'. *quaeque*: 'each woman'.

Line 3: *qua* is used here as the feminine of *quis,* meaning 'any', so 'if any woman ...'.

Line 4: *ea* (antecedent for *quae*) is understood, and is then picked up by the emphatic *illa*: 'she who ..., she (is the one who) ...'. *facit* – context here shows that the sense is 'commit adultery'.

Line 5: *ut* + subjunctive – 'although'. *servaris* is the shortened form of the perfect subjunctive *servaveris*. The perfect tense probably – through its sense of completion – highlights the limit of the action: the husband has kept his wife faithful in physical terms, but this is only worth so much since her desires are (still) adulterous.

Line 6: *custodiri* – this is working as a verb of prevention, hence the *ne* + subjunctive which follows it (NB in this construction the *ne* does not have a negative sense) – 'nor can any woman be kept from ...').

Line 7: *licet* – often followed by *ut* + present subjunctive, but the *ut* can be left out, as here: 'although you may ...'.

Line 9: *licet* + dative + infinitive – impersonal construction = 'it is allowed for *x* to do *y*', so *(ea) cui ... licet* is 'she who is allowed to ...'.

49

Line 11: *desine* + infinitive: 'stop doing *x*'. *vetando*: ablative gerund – 'by forbidding ...'.

Line 12: *aptius* – comparative adverb. *illa* – neuter plural, referring to *vitia*.

Line 14: *ore reluctanti* – not an ablative absolute (notice that the participle ends -*i* not -*e*), but a descriptive ablative: 'his mouth set against the bit'. *fulminis ... modo* : 'like lightning'.

Line 15: *ut primum* – 'as soon as'. Understand *esse* to complete the accusative + infinitive *habenas concessas (esse)*. Scansion shows *effusā*, and so in agreement with *iuba*, following *in*: 'on his streaming mane'.

Line 17: *in* + accusative with a slight sense of purpose, so *nitimur in vetitum*: 'we strive for the forbidden'. *negata* – accusative neuter plural ('the things which are denied').

Line 19: *cervice* – 'on the back of his head'.

Line 20: Argus was a many-eyed giant, appointed fairly fruitlessly by Hera as a guard for the beautiful maiden Io in an attempt to prevent further infidelity by her husband Zeus (see *Metamorphoses* 1 for Ovid's own version of the story). *unus ... Amor* – 'love alone' . For Ovid's use of myth here, and in the lines that follow, see the introduction to this poem.

Lines 21-2: Translate as: *Danae, quae virgo in thalamum ferro saxoque perennem tradita fuerat, mater erat. in thalamum ... perennem ... fuerat ... tradita*: 'had been locked into a room forever strong with ...'. Danaë, while still a virgin, was imprisoned by her father King Acrisius because he had received an oracle that a son born to her would kill him; Zeus, however, got past the locks and bolts by turning himself into a shower of gold, and thus the hero Perseus was conceived.

Line 27: Scansion shows *suā*; both *facie* and *amore* are causal ablatives – 'because of ...'.

Line 28: *ceperit* – subjunctive because part of the indirect speech following *putant*; *nescioquid* is the subject of the infinitive *esse* and the antecedent of *quod*.

Line 29: *cara* – 'prized'.

Line 31: *indignere* = *indigneris* (present subjunctive); *licet indignere* – 'you may get angry' (cf. line 7).

Line 32: *si qua* – see note on line 3. *sola* describes the girl referred to by *qua*.

Line 34: *agat* – jussive subjunctive.

Lines 35-6: *scilicet* adds a scornful tone to the purpose clause, which has as its main clause the deliberative question in line 36 (hence the subjunctive *sit*).

Line 36: *in laudem*: *in* + accusative gives a sense of purpose – 'for the glory...' (see note on line 17).

Line 37: Translate as *is quem coniunx adultera laedit est nimium rusticus*

Line 38: *non satis* with *notos*: *habet ... non satis notos* – 'he does not know well enough ...'. *Urbis* – the capital *U* shows that this refers to Rome.

Lines 39-40: Translate as *in qua Martigenae Romulus Iliades Iliadesque Remus non sine crimine nati sunt*. Romulus and Remus' mother was the Vestal Virgin Rhea Silvia (also known as Ilia), who claimed that Mars was their father, but there was general scepticism (highlighted in Livy's version of the myth) about the truth of her claim and thus the genuineness of her virginity. Even so, these lines must have been shocking to many of Ovid's contemporary readers: for further discussion of this, see the introduction. *Iliades* – Rhea Silvia's alternative name *Ilia* is a reference to Rome's Trojan ancestry: one of Rome's ancient ancestors, Aeneas, had led his men to Italy from Troy (also known as *Ilium*) after their defeat in the Trojan War: these men joined with the Latin people and the Romans were their descendents.

Line 41: *quo* – 'why?'; *quo tibi formosam:* understand something like *elegisti* as the main verb ('why did you choose for yourself ...'); *non nisi* – 'only'.

Line 42: *ista* – neuter plural – refers to the qualities of beauty and chastity.

Line 44: *tuere* – deponent singular imperative (from *tueor*).

Line 45: *amicos* is the object of *cole*; *uxor* belongs in the relative clause *quos dederit*; *dederit* – future perfect indicative but, in keeping with English's tendency to avoid the future tenses in subordinate clauses, better translated as 'she gives'.

Line 48: *dederis* – probably a future perfect indicative, but better translated as 'you have (not) given' – cf. line 45. *domi* – locative ('at home').

Amores 3.5

Introduction

This poem has been the subject of much debate, centred around the question of whether it is actually by Ovid. In order to appreciate this controversy, one must understand the journey that ancient works (or texts) have made from their authors to modern readers in a process known as 'transmission'. All ancient texts which we now have are copies of copies of yet more copies; the author's own original handwritten text (or manuscript) would have been copied by scribes and these texts would then have circulated more widely among the reading public. Before the invention of the printing press, these manuscripts were themselves copied by later readers, whose copies were then copied again, and so on, through many centuries and geographical locations. As anyone who has ever tried to copy a passage by hand knows, it is easy for mistakes to creep in or for syllables, words or even whole sentences to drop out; mistakes therefore tend to accumulate in later copies reliant on manuscripts which themselves contain errors, in a process reminiscent of the game 'Chinese whispers'. Multiple versions of ancient texts therefore ended up circulating in large numbers of different manuscripts, many of which do not derive directly from early manuscripts, and in many cases we cannot be certain about what ancient authors actually wrote – or if they indeed wrote some of the poems which appear among their works.

Amores 3.5 has a highly unusual transmission history: the manuscripts place it in varying locations in the *Amores* collection (some locating it after 3.4, but others in later positions within book three or even in the second book), and while some manuscripts omit the poem altogether, it is also found in manuscripts which contain no other poems from the *Amores*. Such a confused tradition suggests that *Amores* 3.5 did not appear in the earliest copies of the *Amores*, and this has raised suspicions about its authorship.

For lines or sometimes entire poems written in imitation of a famous author (whether as a deliberate forgery or as a creative exercise in composition) sometimes become attached to the manuscripts of authors and transmitted under their name; such texts are 'interpolations', insertions into the textual tradition that are not genuine. As a consequence of suspicions about its authorship, arguments have also been made against this poem being by Ovid on the grounds that it departs from authentically Ovidian works in terms of consistency, language, style, and narrative structure. So, for instance, it is hard to explain why the dream-interpreter is addressed as *quicumque es* at line 31; one might expect Ovid to know this man's identity, given that Ovid has reported his description of his dream to him. However, if the poem lacks internal consistency in this detail, overall it fits well with the interest which *Amores* 3 displays in infidelity and disillusionment with love: compare, for instance, 3.11 and 3.14. There are various apparent linguistic surprises in the poem as well: so, for example, the reference at line 44 to the unfaithful mistress being marked *adulterii labe* ('by the stain of adultery', translated literally) has been seen as suggesting that the cheated poet and the unfaithful mistress of this poem are married to each other, a scenario which would not fit well with the other poems in the *Amores* collection. However, this apparent inconsistency seems less important when we consider that, from Catullus onwards, love poets had presented their extra-marital relationships as equivalent to marriages. Stylistically, Ovid's characteristic pointed use of repetition with variation (for which, see the General Introduction) seems here to be replaced with repetition which sometimes lacks apparent point (e.g. at lines 27-8 and 31-3). Again, scholars are troubled by the fact that it is only at lines 31-2 that we learn that the poem's narrative of a dream is addressed to a dream-interpreter; until this couplet, the poem's dramatic situation has not been clear (contrast 3.2, where the opening line reveals that Ovid is sitting at the races). In modern texts, the inverted commas at the start of the poem hint at the poem's dramatic setting, but because ancient texts lacked punctuation (hence *sic ego*, 33, and *dixerat*, 45, clearly mark the ends of the speeches narrating and interpreting the dream), the poem's dramatic situation is not fully revealed until more than halfway through the poem. We could see this delayed revelation as an oddity that serves no clear artistic purpose. It certainly lacks parallels among genuinely Ovidian works and seems more characteristic of Tibullus, who similarly surprises readers (so, for example, in Tibullus 1.5, we do not learn until lines 67-8 that the entire poem is sung outside the door of the *puella*). Does 3.5 therefore experiment with poetry in the Tibullan manner (after all, *Amores* 3 is clearly interested in Tibullus as Ovid's poetic predecessor, with poem 9 lamenting Tibullus' death) or is this an indication that we are reading the work of an Ovidian imitator? It is impossible to provide a definitive answer. Other people's dreams tend to be boring, but this poem manages not to be, not least because of the many opportunities it offers for debate.

Debates about whether *Amores* 3.5 is interpolated give readers the opportunity to form their own judgement on this question and can also open up valuable discussions about the characteristic features of Ovidian poetry. The poem also has many other interesting aspects, as 3.5 presents us with a novel twist on an earlier elegiac theme, the poet's dream. At Propertius 2.26, for example, Propertius dreams that his mistress, Cynthia, has drowned; by 4.7, Cynthia has apparently died in reality, and Propertius recounts his dream of a visit from her ghost, who attacks him for forgetting her despite his earlier professions that his love would survive beyond the grave. Our poem innovatively combines the unhappy dreams of earlier elegy with the interpretation of the dream's symbolic or allegorical meaning. The dream is explained to the poet (hereafter called Ovid for convenience) as being erotic in nature and meaning that Ovid's *puella* is unfaithful to him. We are still familiar nowadays with the allegorical interpretation of dreams – so, for example, the common dream of one's teeth falling out is now often supposed to symbolise the dreamer's fears of losing their powers. The ancient world was so interested in the allegorical interpretation of dreams that there were professional interpreters of dreams and handbooks on a wide variety of different dream-scenarios. However, the reader of the *Amores* would hardly have to consult an augur (as Ovid does in this poem; the word *augur* usually refers specifically to the interpreter of the behaviour of birds, something which features here at lines 21-4, and is interpreted at 39-40) to recognise that this dream is erotic. Love is, after all, the overriding theme of the *Amores*, and, as we shall see, the details of the dream Ovid narrates (lines 3-30) involve images and language which the reader of elegy is likely to recognise as open to an erotic meaning before such an interpretation is spelled out (at lines 35-44). The skill of *Amores* 3.5 lies in the way in which the dream sets up its interpretation, and much of the pleasure of reading this poem comes from seeing how typical elegiac themes are treated in a novel manner by being recast in the form of a symbolic dream; the reader therefore has the opportunity of questioning the significance and meaning of potentially elegiac elements in the dream. The rest of this essay therefore explores both the dream's use of elegiac themes and their interpretation, before concluding with a brief discussion of the end of the poem.

Suggestively elegiac elements abound from the start. After economically explaining that he was terrified by what he saw in his sleep (1-2; note the very direct opening *Nox erat*, 1), Ovid reveals the particulars of the dream, beginning by locating it in a sunny meadow in which he was seeking refuge from the heat of the day under the trees (3-8). These lines describe a traditional literary *locus amoenus* (or 'pleasant place'; it is worth noting that the first poem of *Amores* 3 opens with a similar sketch of a grove in which Ovid was strolling: a parallel which could suggest authenticity – or imitation). Many of the erotic episodes in Ovid's later *Metamorphoses* are also prefaced with similar scene-setting natural descriptions, which might make the reader suspect that this *locus amoenus* too has erotic overtones. The readers' suspicions might be further aroused by the emphasis on heat (*aestum*, 7, *aestus erat*, 8), later interpreted as the heat of love (35-6), but already a traditional erotic image and one that Ovid had used at *Amores* 3.2.39-40. Despite this hint that the poem is overwhelmingly concerned with Ovidian love, the dream remains on a symbolic rather than literal level: Ovid plays no further part in the action of his dream but relates what he saw in the meadow (9-30). *ecce* (9) provides a dramatic substitute for an actual statement that what follows is a description of what the poet saw in his dream. Ovid sees a shining white (*candida*, 10) heifer accompanied by a bull described as her husband (*maritus*, 15). Emphatic repetition again points to the most significant elements for the interpretation of the dream, as Ovid focuses (i) on the white colouring of the heifer (in the double simile of 11-14), later interpreted as the typical colour of an elegiac *puella* (37), and (ii) on the marital connection of the bull and his mate (with *maritus*, 15, reinforced by *coniuge*, 16). This personification of the animals and the casting of their relationship in marital terms is key to the interpretation of the dream: the bull represents Ovid and the heifer his mistress (38). But the typical elegiac couple do not remain happily together for long and nor do the animals which symbolise them in this poem: the crow which descends (21) and proceeds to peck out some of the heifer's hair (23-4) represents the *lena*, the madam who tries to persuade the elegiac *domina* to leave the elegiac poet-lover for other lovers (39-40; compare, for example, *Amores* 1.8). After the crow's interference, the heifer leaves the bull and seeks *herbae fertilioris humum* (30), a description which suggests that the mistress has followed the *lena*'s advice and is seeking metaphorical pastures new; in the ancient as in the modern world, agricultural images such as this can easily be transferred to erotic situations, as at *Ars amatoria* 1.349, where Ovid suggests that the grass is always greener on the other side.

The interpreter does not, however, spell out the metaphorical potential of line 30's literal description, just as he does not interpret some other erotically suggestive details in the dream. So, for example, the bull is described as chewing the cud *lente* (17), evoking the slow husband who calmly accepts his wife's infidelity (compare *Am.* 2.19.51 and contrast the *Dure vir* of 3.4.1), and the description of the crow as *garrula* (22) suggests the talkativeness of the *lena*; at *Amores* 1.8.23-108, Ovid makes the *lena* deliver a long speech. In that earlier poem, the *lena* had told the *puella* to provoke her lover to jealousy and passion by showing him her neck made *livida* ('discoloured by bruises', *Am.* 1.8.98). In our poem, the heifer similarly has a *niger ... livor* ('black discoloration', 26) left by the crow's pecking. This mark, more symbolic than the literal love-bites of *Amores* 1.8, is here interpreted as the *adulterii labe* (44). What are we to make of the interpreter's failure to interpret such typical elegiac elements? Is this simply a consequence of the dream's interpretation being much shorter than its narration (10 lines as against 28), or the sign of an Ovidian imitator's incompetence? A more illuminating approach to such questions is that the poem thereby provides a challenge to the reader of elegy to make these connections for themselves.

The reader's knowledge of elegy is also helpful in interpreting the concluding lines of the poem, as Ovid responds to the interpreter's speech about the meaning of his dream. In lines 45-6, the blood flees from Ovid's face; the reader of elegy will be aware that turning pale is a common reaction to hearing about the beloved's infidelity (for example, at Ovid's *Ars amatoria* 2.446, 450; compare *Amores* 3.14.38, where Ovid's blood runs cold). Ovid then describes fainting on hearing the dream's interpretation (compare, for example, *Ars amatoria* 2.88), with the nice touch that the night that stands before Ovid's eyes (*ante oculos **nox***) recalls the phrasing of the opening line of the poem: ***Nox** erat, et somnus lassos summisit ocellos*. Ovid's nighttime dream has caused a metaphorical night to overwhelm him as he fears for his relationship with his mistress.

Amores 3.5: Text

'Nox erat, et somnus lassos submisit ocellos;
　　terruerunt animum talia visa meum:
colle sub aprico creberrimus ilice lucus
　　stabat, et in ramis multa latebat avis.
area gramineo suberat viridissima prato　　　　　　　5
　　umida de guttis lene sonantis aquae.
ipse sub arboreis vitabam frondibus aestum,
　　fronde sub arborea sed tamen aestus erat.
ecce petens variis immixtas floribus herbas
　　constitit ante oculos candida vacca meos,　　　　10
candidior nivibus, tum cum cecidere recentes,
　　in liquidas nondum quas mora vertit aquas,
candidior, quod adhuc spumis stridentibus albet
　　et modo siccatam, lacte, reliquit ovem.
taurus erat comes huic, feliciter ille maritus,　　　　15
　　cumque sua teneram coniuge pressit humum.
dum iacet et lente revocatas ruminat herbas
　　atque iterum pasto pascitur ante cibo,
visus erat, somno vires adimente ferendi,
　　cornigerum terra deposuisse caput.　　　　　　20
huc levibus cornix pinnis delapsa per auras
　　venit et in viridi garrula sedit humo
terque bovis niveae petulanti pectora rostro
　　fodit et albentes abstulit ore iubas.
illa locum taurumque diu cunctata reliquit,　　　　25
　　sed niger in vaccae pectore livor erat;
utque procul vidit carpentes pabula tauros
　　(carpebant tauri pabula laeta procul),

illuc se rapuit gregibusque immiscuit illis
    et petiit herbae fertilioris humum.   30
dic age, nocturnae, quicumque es, imaginis augur,
    si quid habent veri, visa quid ista ferant.'
sic ego; nocturnae sic dixit imaginis augur,
    expendens animo singula dicta suo:
'quem tu mobilibus foliis vitare volebas,   35
    sed male vitabas, aestus amoris erat.
vacca puella tua est: aptus color ille puellae;
    tu vir et in vacca compare taurus eras.
pectora quod rostro cornix fodiebat acuto,
    ingenium dominae lena movebit anus;   40
quod cunctata diu taurum sua vacca reliquit,
    frigidus in viduo destituere toro.
livor et adverso maculae sub pectore nigrae
    pectus adulterii labe carere negant.'
dixerat interpres: gelido mihi sanguis ab ore   45
    fugit, et ante oculos nox stetit alta meos.

Amores 3.5: Notes

Line 2: *talia visa* refers forward – 'the following vision'.

Line 3: *sub* + ablative – 'at the foot of'.

Line 4: *multa ... avis* – singular, but in meaning plural (cf. English idiom 'many a bird').

Line 6: *de guttis* – 'with the drops'; *lene sonantis* suggests a quietly trickling stream.

Line 11: *tum cum* – 'at the time when'; *cecidere* is the alternative form of *ceciderunt* (from *cado*); *recentes* – as often in Latin, an adjective in agreement with a verb's subject takes the place of an adverb, so translate as 'freshly'.

Line 12: translate as *quas mora in liquidas aquas nondum vertit.*

Lines 13-14: *lacte* provides the ablative of comparison after *candidior*, and is the antecedent to *quod.*

Line 16: *cum* is a preposition here (+ ablative – *sua ... coniuge*). *humum premere* = to lie upon the ground.

Line 17: *dum* is followed by the present indicative when it means 'at some point during' (see note on 3.2.16), but translate here into a past tense in English.

Line 18: *ante* here is the shortened form of the adverb *antea* and should be taken with *pasto.*

Lines 19-20: *vires ... ferendi* – 'the strength to hold it up'.

Line 20: *terra* – ablative: 'on the ground'.

Line 21: *levibus ... pinnis*: literally 'on light wings', or, more loosely, 'in gentle flight'.

Line 25: *illa* refers to the female cow.

Line 27: *ut* + indicative – 'when ...'.

Line 28: *laeta*: *laetus* has as its basic meaning 'rich' or 'fertile' and should be translated thus here.

Line 29: *se rapere* = to hasten; *gregibusque (se) immiscuit illis* – 'and joined those herds'.

Line 30: *petiit* = *petivit; herbae fertilioris* – descriptive genitive, so 'with richer grass'.

Lines 31-2: *dic age* – 'come on, tell me'. *veri* is a partitive genitive after *siquid*: 'if ... any truth'. *visa quid ista ferant* – indirect question after *dic age*: 'what those things I saw mean'.

Lines 35-6: understand *aestus* as the antecedent for *quem*.

Line 37: *aptus color ille puellae* – understand *est*.

Line 38: understand *es* with *vir* ('lover').

Line 39: *quod* here is 'as for the fact that'; translate as: *quod cornix pectora rostro acuto fodiebat*.

Line 40: *lena* refers to a brothel's keeper or madam; in conjunction with *anus* could be translated as 'a brothel's hag ...' . *ingenium ... movebit* – 'will influence the mind'.

Line 41: *quod* – 'as for the fact that' (cf. line 39). Sometimes the reflexive pronoun / adjective takes as its reference the focus of the sentence rather than the grammatical subject, so *taurum sua vacca reliquit* = 'his own cow left the bull'.

Line 42: *destituere* – alternative form of the future passive *destitueris*.

Line 43: *adverso* – 'in front of you'.

Line 44: *negant* + infinitive – best translated as 'mean that ... not ...' . The repetition of *pectus* highlights the parallels between dream and reality, but this repetition is hard to match in English since in line 43 the meaning is 'chest', and in line 44 'heart'.

Amores 3.14

Introduction

Amores 3.14 is the last elegy in the *Amores* to treat a 'personal' erotic scenario; the next (and final) poem, *Amores* 3.15, bids farewell to love elegy, as Ovid announces his intention to pursue more weighty poetic projects. As the penultimate *Amores* poem and the final elegy in the collection concerned with the theme of elegiac love, our poem looks back to earlier *Amores* poems and the broader tradition of erotic poetry. The basic scenario of the poem, set out epigrammatically in its first couplet, is that Ovid, aware of his mistress' infidelities towards him, tries to persuade her to spare his feelings by keeping her other liaisons secret. The next couplet sums up: Ovid demands not that his mistress be chaste (*pudica*, 3) but that she should attempt to conceal her bad behaviour (*temptes dissimulare*, 4). Two major concerns of this *suasoria* (for this term, see the General Introduction) are therefore sexual morality and deception, and the poem is particularly interesting for the way in which Ovid exploits earlier erotic poetry in handling these themes. Another important element of the poem is the extent to which it portrays jealousy and erotic suffering in a realistic or serious manner. These aspects of *Amores* 3.14 are treated in the introduction to the poem which follows, which closes with a discussion of *Amores* 3.14's role as the final erotic poem of the *Amores* collection.

Given the basic set-up to the poem – that Ovid's mistress has been deceiving him with other men – we might expect *Amores* 3.14 to present us with a jealous, suffering lover. In fact, Ovid's acceptance of his mistress' behaviour – indeed, the way in which he gives her advice on how best to deceive him – does not suggest a man profoundly in love, and we learn nothing about the happier times in this relationship; Ovid focuses instead on his mistress's behaviour in bed with another man (see further below).

This tacit acceptance of the mistress's unfaithfulness is at odds with the pain expressed over such infidelity in other love poems, such as *Amores* 3.11, where a jealous Ovid even attempts to give up on love, before declaring that he cannot live with – or without – his mistress. *Amores* 3.11 anticipates our poem in talking about the way in which hatred and love are simultaneously aroused by the mistress's misbehaviour (compare line 39 *tunc amo, tunc odi frustra, quod amare necesse est* with *Amores* 3.11.33-4 *luctantur pectusque leve in contraria tendunt/ hac amor hac odium, sed, puto, vincit amor*, 'hatred and love struggle and pull my fickle heart in opposite directions, but, I think, love has the upper hand') , a motif that comes from Catullus 85, whose single elegiac couplet treats the same erotic dilemma: *Odi et amo. quare id faciam, fortasse requiris?/ nescio, sed fieri sentio et excrucior* ('I hate and I love. Why do I do that, perhaps you ask? I do not know, but I feel it happening to me and I am tortured'). Our poem seems much less anguished than these earlier love poems expressing similar sentiments; whereas Catullus 85 attempts to analyse his contradictory feelings, declares his powerlessness over them, and expresses the resulting torture that he feels, this is very different from Ovid telling his mistress that he is willing to be fooled by her, and our poem's play with the paradox that Ovid is well aware that self-deception must play a part in his lack of knowledge of his mistress' infidelities (see particularly 45-6). The lack of suffering in this poem compared with others on similar themes is highlighted when Ovid makes what is surely the most extreme statement of our poem, the claim that his emotions make him want to die, *sed tecum* ('but with you', 40). Propertius had already treated the gruesome theme of the poet's murder of his mistress, followed by his own suicide, in 2.8, declaring that 'you will not escape; you must die with me; let the blood of us both drip from this same sword' (25-6), but the murder-suicide theme, which in Propertius encapsulates his over-the-top, emotionally extreme rhetoric as a lover, hardly seems serious at all in Ovid, as *sed tecum* reduces the murder of the mistress to a brief, throwaway comment. The lack of seriousness of Ovid's threat is compounded by the bathos of the couplet which follows, in which Ovid sees being deceived by his mistress as a favour (41-2). Our poem is not so much about the lover's mental anguish as about the contradiction of the lover demanding that his mistress deceive him, in full knowledge of the fact that he is being deceived.

It had been clear from as early as *Amores* 1.4 that deception plays an important role in Ovidian love affairs: in that poem, Ovid advises a woman on how to flirt secretly with Ovid while at a dinner party, concealing their affair from her *vir*. Towards the end of *Amores* 1.4, Ovid reluctantly accepts that his mistress will leave the dinner party with his rival, her *vir*, to spend the night with him, yet Ovid insists that his mistress should afterwards tell him that she has refused her *vir*'s erotic advances, *whether this is true or not*. Deception in the *Amores*, then, is not simply a matter of Ovid deceiving his rivals or his mistress; Ovid himself also needs to be deceived. Although the basic premise of our poem is that Ovid is upset at his mistress' current behaviour, the fact that he asks her not to amend her ways but to conceal her infidelities from him (and gives her advice on how to continue her affairs with discretion) makes the reader question just how seriously we should take this poem as an expression of erotic suffering. It would be easy to accordingly dismiss the poem as a literary and intellectual exercise in exploring sexual jealousy, but the poem seems at least psychologically convincing: people *do* deceive themselves in order to stay in relationships (and Ovid's interest in psychological realism is evident from poems such as his *Heroides* or *Metamorphoses*, which depict various mythical characters in extreme states of mind). The lover who is aware of his mistress' infidelity but chooses to overlook it in full knowledge of her behaviour also has good precedents in earlier Latin love poetry: for example, in his elegiac poem 68, Catullus had noted that his mistress was 'not satisfied with Catullus alone' (*uno non est contenta Catullo*, 135), but declared that 'I shall bear the occasional illicit affairs of my discreet mistress' (*rara verecundae furta feremus erae*, 136), and Propertius 2.32 had also treated the theme of tolerating the mistress' infidelities. Ovid develops the theme of tolerance of the mistress' sexual misbehaviour by spelling out the self-deception that this involves for the lover who manages to stay in a relationship with such a woman.

Concepts of female sexual propriety lie at the heart of this poem, which is much concerned with the discussion of *pudor* ('a sense of shame/ modesty'; the word is often used with reference to women's sexual behaviour, as here), a quality which Ovid wishes his mistress would *pretend* to have. After the two opening couplets sum up the poem's basic premise, Ovid moves to complaints about his mistress' lack of concealment of her liaisons (5-12), claiming that what is problematic is not sexual infidelity itself but rather the broadcasting of such misbehaviour (5-6). Ovid's mistress has apparently been very indiscreet: Ovid implies that she is less concerned with her reputation than a prostitute (*meretrix*, 9), since prostitutes at least conceal their sexual encounters behind bolted doors (10). The idea of prostitution is continued in the next couplet, with *prostitues* (11); the literal meaning of this verb is 'to prostitute', but Ovid here uses it in the rare sense of 'to expose to public shame' as he focuses on his mistress' lack of shame about her sexual exploits (while simultaneously hinting, thanks to the literal connotations, that his mistress is as sexually available as a prostitute). Augustan morality is relevant to these lines, since sex with prostitutes did not come under the scope of Augustus' anti-adultery law (for which, see further the General Introduction); Ovid's comparison of his (unnamed) mistress' behaviour with that of a prostitute strongly implies that she is *not* in fact a prostitute. The logical conclusion is that the wanton sexual behaviour whose display Ovid deplores here is therefore illegal. Ovid again problematically evokes the Augustan anti-adultery law at line 12 when he refers to his mistress giving evidence of her own sexual misbehaviour; Ovid seems to have invented the elegiac role of the *index* (or 'informer') who gives evidence about adulterous affairs, as people were encouraged to do by Augustus' moral legislation. The paradox of the wanton woman of this poem acting as informer on *her own* infidelities shows how foolish Ovid believes her behaviour to be (indeed, at line 7, confession of acts which ought to be private is labelled *furor* or 'madness'). This leads Ovid to suggest again that his mistress at least pretend to be chaste (13-14), and to a discussion of the appropriateness of wanton behaviour to the bedroom but not in public (17-28). The *appearance* of respectability is what matters, not respectable behaviour itself (27), but Ovid's mistress' flagrant conduct does not allow him to believe that she is respectable: lines 31-4 detail the evidence of his mistress' affairs which Ovid has seen with his own eyes, recalling earlier love elegy. For instance, the notes sent on tablets (*tabellas*, 31) recall *Amores* 1.11 and 12, paired poems in which Ovid asks a slave to carry a message to Corinna setting up an assignation (1.11) and in which Ovid bemoans Corinna's reply turning him down (1.12); the love-bite (*dentis ... notam*, 34) Ovid sees on the mistress' neck commonly features in elegy. Ovid appears more upset by his mistress flaunting her misbehaviour (35) than by her actions themselves, although the fact that she virtually brings her crime before Ovid's eyes (35) leads him to discuss the physical and emotional effects that this situation has upon him (37-40; compare the reference to Ovid fainting at the end of *Amores* 3.5). Ovid ends the poem by restating his willingness to overlook his mistress' behaviour and to be deceived (41-50), in a passage which is striking for its sustained use of legalistic language and concepts (for Ovid's legal experience and its influence on his poetry, see the General Introduction). Although legal vocabulary occurs throughout the poem (for example, *pecces*, 1, *culpa*, 6, *commissi ... indicium*, 12, and *crimen*, 20, 27, 35 can all have legal applications), it clusters particularly at the end of the poem, which talks about Ovid's mistress being caught in the act (*in media deprensa tenebere culpa*, 43), tells her to defend herself with a plea which might more naturally come from a defendant in court (*'non feci'*, 48), refers to her *causa* ('(legal) case', 50), and suggests that Ovid is the judge of her behaviour (*iudice ... tuo*, 50), albeit one who is inclined to let her off. What are we to make of such repeated use of legal vocabulary and concepts? Does it add *gravitas* ('seriousness') to the poem? Does the behaviour of Ovid's mistress seem more shocking because it is described in legal terminology? Might Ovid even be satirising the idea that sexual behaviour is subject to the law (with obvious implications for the Augustan moral legislation)?

Although our poem is very concerned with imposing Ovid's idea of proper conduct on his mistress, much of its content is at odds both with the pose of judge which Ovid adopts and with conventional morality. The poem therefore provides a good illustration of elegy's rejection of accepted standards (for which, see further the General Introduction); I consider below several examples from the many that could be adduced. Ovid's opening statement that he does not demand that his mistress should be chaste 'since you are beautiful' (*cum sis formosa*, 1) shows the unorthodox values of the elegiac world, where promiscuity is the natural prerogative of the beautiful woman and the Augustan moral legislation is simply irrelevant. Again, the claim that *non peccat, quaecumque potest peccasse negare* (5) goes against normal distinctions between right and wrong: the repetition of the verb *peccare* ('to commit a moral offence'; often used with reference to adultery or sexual peccadilloes) undermines the sense of morality inherent in the word, since Ovid here makes wrongdoing a matter merely of *getting caught out*, with denial always an option. Ovid pokes more obvious fun at conventional standards at line 16, turning morality on its head when he advises *nec pudeat coram verba modesta loqui*. The surprising idea that a woman might be ashamed of speaking *modest* words is so far from what is expected (i.e. shame at speaking *immodest* words) that the effect is humorous. Further outrage is done to convention at line 27, where respectability is something that can be put on with your clothes when you leave the bedroom. Ovid here employs one of his favourite literary devices, syllepsis (where the same verb is used with both a literal and a metaphorical sense; here, *induo* means both to 'put on' clothes and 'assume' an appearance), and the effect is humorous, while amoral. A final aspect of the topsy-turvy morality of this poem that demands discussion is the passage on the behaviour appropriate to the bedroom (17-26), a location where Ovid claims that *pudor* is not expected, and wantonness is called for (17-18). There is a distinct lack of *pudor* to Ovid's description of the activities which take place in the bedroom: although Ovid follows the conventions of love elegy in avoiding lexically offensive terms (i.e. four-letter words), this passage contains more sexually explicit material than most elegiac poems. So, for instance, sex is clearly implied in line 22, where the different cases of the word *femur* ('thigh') suggest bodies coming together in intercourse, although Ovid eschews more anatomically specific language. The reference to kissing in line 23 could be seen as innocent enough, but the same cannot be said of the reference in the following line to *modos venerem mille*, alluding to multiple sexual positions. Ovid's fairly graphic description of sex in this passage concentrates on the pleasure of those involved, and undermines the idea that he is deeply hurt by his mistress' sexual encounters with others; indeed, the jussive subjunctives found in lines 21-6 may even encourage his mistress' uninhibited sexual behaviour.

Finally, it is worth considering how our poem functions as a conclusion to the erotic, personal poetry of the three books of the *Amores*. Given the disillusionment that Ovid expresses in this poem about the game of elegiac love, a game that has forced him to accept his mistress' infidelities and find a way of dealing with them, *Amores* 3.14 may seem like a fitting conclusion to the love poems of the *Amores*, a 'farewell' to love. However, Ovid does not explicitly say here that his disenchantment with his own experience of love has led him to abandon love. The poem thus forms a strong contrast to the concluding poems (3.24 and 25) of Propertius' third book of elegies, which clearly signpost the end of Propertius' love affair with Cynthia, revisiting in detail the opening poem of Propertius 1 as Propertius finally repudiates his erotic infatuation with one woman. Instead, here, as in other poems of the *Amores*, Ovid playfully develops an erotic theme which had been treated in earlier love poetry. Indeed, Ovid never wholly rejects love elegy, but rather takes it in new directions in his later writing: for example, treating it as a code which can be taught in the *Ars amatoria*, or adapting its typical situations and complaints and putting them into the mouths of mythical heroines in his *Heroides*. Given Ovid's concern with producing an innovative version of love elegy in the *Amores* (something which the poems in this current volume abundantly demonstrate), this should come as little surprise to the reader.

Amores 3.14: Text

Non ego, ne pecces, cum sis formosa, recuso,
    sed ne sit misero scire necesse mihi;
nec te nostra iubet fieri censura pudicam
    sed tamen ut temptes dissimulare rogat.
non peccat, quaecumque potest peccasse negare,   5
    solaque famosam culpa professa facit.
quis furor est, quae nocte latent, in luce fateri
    et, quae clam facias, facta referre palam?
ignoto meretrix corpus iunctura Quiriti
    opposita populum submovet ante sera;   10
tu tua prostitues famae peccata sinistrae
    commissi perages indiciumque tui?
sit tibi mens melior, saltemve imitare pudicas,
    teque probam, quamvis non eris, esse putem.
quae facis, haec facito: tantum fecisse negato   15
    nec pudeat coram verba modesta loqui.
est qui nequitiam locus exigat: omnibus illum
    deliciis inple, stet procul inde pudor.
hinc simul exieris, lascivia protinus omnis
    absit, et in lecto crimina pone tuo.   20
illic nec tunicam tibi sit posuisse pudori
    nec femori inpositum sustinuisse femur;
illic purpureis condatur lingua labellis,
    inque modos venerem mille figuret amor;
illic nec voces nec verba iuvantia cessent,   25
    spondaque lasciva mobilitate tremat.
indue cum tunicis metuentem crimina vultum,
    et pudor obscenum diffiteatur opus.

da populo, da verba mihi: sine nescius errem
    et liceat stulta credulitate frui.   30
cur totiens video mitti recipique tabellas?
    cur pressus prior est interiorque torus?
cur plus quam somno turbatos esse capillos
    collaque conspicio dentis habere notam?
tantum non oculos crimen deducis ad ipsos;   35
    si dubitas famae parcere, parce mihi.
mens abit et morior, quotiens peccasse fateris,
    perque meos artus frigida gutta fluit.
tunc amo, tunc odi frustra, quod amare necesse est;
    tunc ego, sed tecum, mortuus esse velim.   40
nil equidem inquiram nec, quae celare parabis,
    insequar: et falli muneris instar erit.
si tamen in media deprensa tenebere culpa
    et fuerint oculis probra videnda meis,
quae bene visa mihi fuerint, bene visa negato: 45
    concedent verbis lumina nostra tuis.
prona tibi vinci cupientem vincere palma est,
    sit modo 'non feci' dicere lingua memor:
cum tibi contingat verbis superare duobus,
    etsi non causa, iudice vince tuo.   50

Amores 3.14: Notes

Line 1: *recuso* here is followed by *ne* + present subjunctive (cf. the standard construction for verbs of hindering / preventing where *ne* similarly has no negative sense), and so *non recuso ne pecces* – 'I do not object to your infidelity'; *cum* here means 'since'.

Line 2: *ne sit ... necesse* – also follows recuso: '... but (I do object) that it is necessary ...'.

Line 3: *nostra* – poetic plural for singular, so translate as *mea*.

Line 5: *peccasse* = *peccavisse*; understand *se* with *peccasse,* both after *negare.*

Line 6: *sola ... culpa professa* – all in agreement. *professa* (from *profiteor*) has a reflexive sense of 'having declared itself', and so in better English 'admitted'.

Lines 7-8: *quis furor est ... fateri et ... referre palam* – 'what madness is it to confess ... and to tell openly ... '. Understand *ea* as the antecedent to *quae* (line 7) and the object of *fateri*; *facta* is the object of *referre* and the antecedent of *quae* (line 8). *facias* – subjunctive in a generic *qui*-clause, i.e. a clause where the relative pronoun has the meaning 'the sort ... which ...'.

Line 9: *corpus iunctura* – 'about to make love to'.

Line 10: *ante* = *antea* and so the ablative absolute *opposita ... ante sera* means 'having bolted the door first'.

Line 11: *prostitues* – 'will you expose'; *famae ... sinistrae* – 'unfavourable gossip'.

Line 13: *sit* – jussive subjunctive; *imitare* – deponent imperative (singular).

Line 14: *quamvis non eris* – as for most subordinate clauses that refer to the future, the future indicative is best translated into a present tense in English (cf. future temporal and conditional clauses); *putem* – jussive subjunctive.

Line 15: *quae* – neuter plural, and so the object of *facis. facito ... negato* – both are future imperatives, broadly equivalent to the standard (present) imperative: the future imperative is slightly more formal, and is often used in legal documents, laws, maxims and so on. Understand *te* with *fecisse*, both following on from *negato*. For more on the legal nuances of much of this poem, see the introduction.

Line 16: *nec* for *neu* (= *et ne*). *pudeat* – jussive subjunctive.

Line 17: Translate as *est locus qui nequitiam exigat*; *exigat* – subjunctive in a generic *qui*-clause (see note on lines 7-8).

Line 18: *stet* – jussive subjunctive.

Line 19: *exieris* – future perfect indicative, but translate as a perfect tense in English since the future tenses are rarely used in English subordinate clauses (cf. line 14).

Line 20: *absit* – jussive subjunctive. *pone* – 'leave'.

Line 21: *pudori* – predicative dative: *nec tibi sit pudori* – 'let it be no shame to you'.

Line 23: *condatur* – jussive subjunctive. *labellum* is the diminutive of *labrum*, and so gives an indulgent tone to the line.

Line 24: *figuret* – jussive subjunctive; *mille* with *modos; venerem* – 'passion / love-making'.

Line 25: *cessent* – jussive subjunctive.

Line 26: *lasciva* – scansion shows this to be ablative (with *mobilitate*).

Line 28: *diffiteatur* – jussive subjunctive.

Line 29: *da ... verba* – 'tell lies'; *sine ... errem* is a shortened form of *sine ut* + subjunctive – 'allow that ...'.

Line 30: *liceat* (jussive subjunctive) + the infinitive *frui* – 'let it be possible to enjoy ...'. Note that *fruor* takes the ablative case.

Line 32: as is common, the adjectives (*prior* and *interior*) agreeing with the verb's subject are best translated as adverbs: 'why has your bed been pressed hard upon before and rather intimately?'

Line 33: *plus quam somno*: 'more than by sleep'.

Line 34: *colla* – poetic plural for singular (cf. line 3).

Line 35: *tantum non ...* – 'the only thing you do not do is ...'.

Line 37: understand *te* with *peccasse fateris. peccasse* is the shortened form of *peccavisse*.

Line 39: *quod* – 'because'.

Line 40: *velim* – 'I should like'.

Lines 41-2: understand *ea* as object of *insequar* and antecedent to *quae*; *parabis* is best translated into the present tense in English (cf. lines 14 and 19). *falli* – present passive infinitive; it can often be best to translate the infinitive as a noun, especially when it is the subject of a sentence, so here 'deception'.

Line 43: *tenebere* is the alternative form of the future passive *teneberis*; the future tense in a conditional clause is best translated as a present tense in English (cf. lines 14, 19 and 41-2). *deprensa* – 'red-handed'.

Line 44: *videnda* is the gerundive of obligation; the future perfect *fuerint* gives a sense of completion to the action, but as part of the conditional clause is best translated as a present tense, so '... must be seen'.

Line 45: Translate as *negato ea, quae bene visa mihi fuerint, bene visa esse. negato* is a future imperative form (cf. line 15); *bene visa* – 'clearly seen'; *fuerint* is subjunctive since it is in a subordinate clause in indirect speech – translate as a normal perfect tense; the dative *mihi* is used instead of the more usual *a(b)* + ablative and brings with it the nuance that the action had an impact on the agent (cf. the usual construction after a gerundive of obligation).

Line 46: *nostra* – poetic plural for singular (cf. lines 3 and 34); *lumina nostra* refers to Ovid's eyes as witness to the girl's behaviour – the meaning is that he will ignore the evidence of what he has seen and believe her words instead.

Line 47: *palma* is the palm-branch given to a winner (see *Amores* 3.2 line 82), so *prona tibi ... palma est* – 'it is an easy victory for you ...'; *vinci cupientem* – 'one who longs to be won-over'.

Line 48: *sit* – jussive subjunctive; *memor esse* + infinitive – 'remember to'.

Line 49: *cum* introduces here a causal clause, in which the subjunctive (*contingat*) is used – 'since ...' . *contingat* – used impersonally here (+ dative + infinitive).

Line 50: *etsi non* – 'even if not'; *causa* – 'because of your case'; *iudice tuo* (like *causa*) is ablative to express the means of victory, so 'because of your judge'.

Appendix
Translation of *Amores* 2.19

If you feel no personal need of guarding your girl, fool,
    at least guard her for me so that I might love her more.
What is permitted is unpleasing; what is not permitted burns more
                                                    fiercely:
    he is hard-hearted, the man who loves what another man allows.
Let us lovers hope simultaneously, let us fear simultaneously,
    and let an occasional rejection give the opportunity for prayer.
Why should I wish for a fortune which never cared to deceive me?
    I love nothing which does not hurt at some point.
Wily Corinna had observed this fault in me,
    and craftily got to know the means by which I could be captured.
Ah, how often having feigned a headache
    she ordered me, dragging my feet, to depart!
Ah, how often she pretended an offence, and as much as she could
                                                    with an innocent,
    provided the appearance that I was guilty!
So when she had disturbed me and rekindled lukewarm fires,
    again she was obliging and fitting to my prayers.
What blandishments, what sweet words she kept granting me!
    The kisses (good gods!) – what kind and how many she kept giving!
You too, who have recently captured my eyes,
    often fear traps; often, having been propostioned, refuse,
and allow me, stretched out on the threshold before your doorposts,
    to suffer the lengthy cold on a frosty night.
So my love endures and grows strong for long years;
    this pleases, these are the things that nourish my emotions.
A rich love and one that is too easy turns to boredom for me,
    and harms my stomach, like sweet food.

If a bronze tower had never held Danaë,
    Danaë would not have been made a mother by Jove.
While Juno was guarding Io, transformed with horns,
    Io was made more welcome than she had previously been to Jove.
Whoever desires what is permitted and easy would pluck leaves
    from a tree and drink water from a great river;
if any woman desires to reign for a long time, let her deceive her lover
    (alas me, may I not be tortured by my own advice!).
Whatever may happen, indulgence is harmful to me:
    I flee what pursues; what flees, I myself pursue.
But you, too secure in a beautiful girl,
    begin now to close the door at nightfall;
begin to ask who so often knocks at your door secretly,
    and why the dogs bark in the silent night,
what letters the resourceful maidservant carries back and forth,
    why so often your wife sleeps apart on an empty couch.
Let this care eventually gnaw at your marrows,
    and give me an opportunity and reason for tricks.
That man is able to thieve sand from the empty shore
    who is able to love the wife of a fool.
And now I warn you: unless you begin to guard your girl,
    she will cease to be mine.
I've endured a lot and for a long time: often I hoped that,
    when you had guarded her well, I would deceive well.
You are slow to react, allow things that are acceptable to no husband;
    Permitted love will be the end of love for me.
Am I really, unlucky man, never to be prevented from approaching?
    Will I always have a night without any consequences?
Shall I fear nothing? Sigh no sighs in my sleep?
    Will you give me no good reason to wish you dead?
What business have I with an indulgent husband, one who is a pimp?
    He destroys my pleasures with his fault.
Why not look for someone who wants such great forbearance?
    If it pleases you to have me as a rival, shut me out.

Vocabulary

abdo -dere -didi -ditum to remove, to hide
acūtus -a -um sharp, piercing, painful
adhūc still
adimo -imere -ēmi -emptum to take away
admitto -mittere -mīsi -missum to send to, let in (*when used of horses*:
    to let go, put to a gallop)
admoveo -movēre -mōvi -mōtum to move to, bring to
adnuo -nuere -nui -nūtum (+*dat*) to nod assent to, approve of
adsurgo -surgere -surrexi -surrectum to rise up, stand up
adulter -era -erum adulterous
adulter -eri, m adulterer
adultera -ae, f adulteress
adulterium -i, n adultery
aeger -gra -grum invalid, sick
aequus -a -um equal, level, fair
āēr āeris, m air
aestus -ūs, m heat, agitation, excitement
agitātor -ōris, m driver, charioteer
agmen -inis, n column, line (of men, or any other mass in movement)
albeo -ēre to be white
albus -a -um white
altus -a -um high, deep
an or (often follows a clause where there is some sense of doubt – *or is
    it then…*)
ante (+*acc*) before
anteā previously, before
anus -ūs, f old woman
aprīcus -a -um sunny
aptus -a -um (+*dat*) fitting, suitable
arboreus -a -um of a tree
arcesso -ere -īvi -ītum to summon

arcus -ūs, m bow
ardeo ardēre arsi to burn, be on fire
ārea -ae, f level / open space
Argus i, m Argus, a hundred-eyed giant
argūtus -a -um expressive, lively
arma -ōrum, n armour, weapons
artifex -icis skilled, creative
artus -ūs, m: *in plural* joints, limbs
at but, moreover
Atalantē -ēs, f Atalanta (a Greek maiden famous for her speed in running, unbeaten in a race until Milanion overtook her, and then married her)
aufero auferre abstuli ablātum to take away, steal
augur -uris, m/f augur (interpreter of omens, especially birds)
aura -ae, f breeze, air
aureus -a -um golden
avis -is, f bird
axis -is, m wheel axle

Bacchus -i, m Bacchus (god of wine and the vine)
blandus -a -um alluring, enticing, flattering
bōs bovis, m/f ox, bull, cow

cado cadere cecidi cāsum to fall down
cancelli -ōrum, m pl grating
candidus -a -um bright / shining white
capillus -i, m hair
carcer -eris, m prison, *here:* starting-place in a racecourse
careo -ēre -ui (*+abl*) to be without
carpo carpere carpsi carptum to pluck, take, eat, graze on
cārus -a -um dear, beloved, high-priced
Castor -oris, m Castor (twin brother of the god Pollux)
castus -a -um chaste, faithful, morally pure
causa -ae, f cause, reason, legal case
cēdo cēdere cessi cessum to go away, retire
cēlo -are to hide, keep secret

censūra -ae, f criticism

centum a hundred

Cerēs -eris, f Ceres (goddess of agriculture)

cervix -īcis, f neck, nape of the neck

cibus -i, m food

circueo (= circumeo) -ire -uii -itum to go round

circus -i, m racecourse

clam secretly

claudo claudere clausi clausum to shut, close, make inaccessible

coeo -īre -ii -itum to go / come together, unite, combine

cōgo cōgere coēgi coactum to force, compel

colligo -ligere -lēgi -lectum to gather together

collis collis, m hill

collum -i, n neck

colo colere colui cultum to take care of, respect, honour

color -ōris, m colour

comes -itis, m/f companion

commissum -i, m crime, fault, transgression

commodus -a -um convenient, appropriate, obliging

concedo -cēdere -cessi -cessum to yield, withdraw, give in to, agree to

concido -cidere -cidi to fall down to the ground, collapse, perish

conditus -a -um hidden

condo condere condidi condītum to hide, bury

coniunx -iugis, f wife

conpar –paris, m/f companion, mate

consisto -sistere -stiti -stitum to stand (still), halt

contactus -ūs, m touch, contact

contingo -tingere -tigi -tactum (*+dat*) touch, *intrans* (*+dat*) to happen, befall

contrā (*+acc*) against

contraho -trahere -traxi -tractum to draw together, draw in

convīvium -i, n banquet, party

cōram openly

corniger -gera -gerum horned

cornix -īcis, f crow

corpus corporis, n body

crēber -bra -brum thick, full of
crēdulitās -ātis, f credulity, readiness to believe
crīmen -inis, n accusation, fault, guilt, crime
crūs crūris, n shin, leg
culpa -ae, f blame, fault
cunctor -ari to delay, hesitate, linger
cūra -ae, f care, concern
cursus -ūs, m race
custos -ōdis, m guard, watchman

Danaē -ēs, f Danaë (a maiden shut up in a bronze tower by her father, King Acrisius, who had heard in a prophecy that a son of hers would kill him)
dēdūco -dūcere -duxi -ductum to lead / bring down
dēlābor -lābi -lapsus sum to glide / fall down
dēliciae -ārum, f pl charms, delights
dēmo dēmere dempsi demptum to take away
dēnique at last, in short
dens dentis, m tooth
dēpōno -pōnere -posui -positum to put down, lay aside
dēprehendo / dēprendo -endere -endi -ensum to seize upon, catch hold of, surprise
dēsino -sinere -sii -situm to cease, stop doing
dēstituo -stituere -stitui -stitūtum to leave behind, forsake, desert
dextra -ae, f the right hand
Diāna -ae, f Diana (the Roman equivalent of the Greek Artemis, goddess of chastity and hunting)
diffiteor -ēri to deny
digitus -i, m finger
discolor -ōris of different colours
dīvus -a -um divine (*used as a noun:* god / goddess)
domus -ūs, f home
dubito -are to doubt, hesitate
dum while, during, until
dūrus -a -um hard, harsh, severe

effundo -fundere -fūdi -fūsum to pour forth / out
en look! see!
enim indeed
eques -itis, m horseman, member of the cavalry
equidem indeed, for my part
ergō therefore
erro -are to stray, lose one's way, make a mistake
ēvolo -are to fly forth, rush out
exigo -igere -ēgi -actum to drive out, force out, demand
expendo -pendere -pendi -pensum to weigh out / up, consider
externus -a -um external, foreign, strange
exuo -uere -ui -ūtum to take off, put aside

faciēs -ēi, f shape, form, appearance
fallo fallere fefelli falsum to deceive, cheat, escape the notice of
fāma -ae, f rumour, reputation
fāmōsus -a -um much spoken of, notorious
fateor fatēri fassus sum to confess, reveal
faveo favēre fāvi fautum (+*dat*) to favour, support
favor -ōris, n support, favour
fēlīciter fruitfully, luckily, successfully
fēlix -īcis lucky, successful
fēmineus -a -um of a woman, for a woman
femur -oris, n thigh
fera -ae, f wild animal
ferrum -i, n iron
fertilis -e fruitful, prolific, fertile
figūro -are to form, shape
fīo fieri factus sum to become, happen
flamma -ae, f flame
flōs flōris, m flower
fluo -ere fluxi fluxum to flow, pour
fodio fodere fōdi fossum to dig, dig out, pluck
folium -i, n leaf
formōsus -a -um beautifully formed, beautiful
forte by chance

frēna -ōrum, n pl bridle, reins
frīgidus -a -um cold, icy, chilling
frons frondis, f leaf, foliage
frons frontis, f forehead, brow
fruor frui fructus sum (+*abl*) to enjoy
frustrā in vain
fugax -ācis on the run, fleeing
fulmen -inis, n stroke of lightning, thunderbolt
fundo fundere fūdi fūsum to pour
fūr, fūris, m thief
furor -ōris, m madness, passion

garrulus -a -um chattering, talkative
gelidus -a -um icy
gens gentis, f race, nation
genu -ūs, n knee
gero gerere gessi gessum to wear, carry about, conduct
gramineus -a -um grassy
grātia -ae, f popularity, influence
grex gregis, m herd
gutta -ae, f drop, droplet

habēna -ae, f strap, bridle, rein
hasta -ae, f spear
herba -ae, f grass, green shoots
hinc from here
Hippodamīa -ae, f Hippodamia (daughter of Oenomaus)
hūc hither, to here
humus -i, f ground, earth

iaceo iacēre iacui to lie, lie down / upon, hang loosely
iacto -are to throw / fling off
ignāvus -a -um lazy, cowardly, good for nothing
ignōtus -a -um unknown
īlex -icis, f holm-oak
Īliadēs -ae, m son of Ilia (Romulus and Remus' mother)

illīc in / at that place
illūc thither
imāgo -inis, f image, ghost, dream
imitor -ari to imitate, copy
immineo -ēre to overhang, hang over
incipio -cipere -cēpi -ceptum to begin
inconcessus -a -um forbidden
inde from there
indicium -i, n evidence
indignor -ari to consider unworthy, to be indignant at
indulgeo -dulgēre -dulsi (+*dat*) to be indulgent towards
induo -duere -dui -dūtum to put on, clothe
infēlix -īcis unlucky, unhappy, miserable
ingenium -i, n nature, temperament, talent, ability
ingenuus -a -um free-born, honourable, delicate
inmisceo -miscēre -miscui -mixtum to intermingle, join with
inmixtus -a -um intermingled, mixed together
inpleo -plēre -plēvi -plētum (+*dat*) to fill up, fill full
inpōno -pōnere -posui -positum to put in position, put upon
inquīro -quīrere -quīsīvi -quīsītum to search, look for
inrīto -are to stir up, excite
insequor -sequi -secūtus sum to follow after, follow up, pursue, reproach
insero -serere -serui -sertum to insert
insisto -sistere -stiti (+*dat*) to follow hard upon
instar (+*gen*) equivalent to
insurgo -surgere -surrexi -surrectum to rise up against, to increase in power / force
intemerātus -a -um undefiled, untouched
interdīco -dīcere -dixi -dictum to forbid, prohibit, outlaw
intereā meanwhile
interior -ius inner, more intimate
interpres –prētis, m/f someone who explains, a prophet, soothsayer, interpreter
intus inside
invidus -a -um envious

iste, ista, istud that, that one right there
iterum again
iuba -ae, f mane, tuft of hair
iūdex -icis, m judge
iungo iungere iunxi iunctum to join, unite
iūro -are to swear (an oath)
iūs iūris, n right, law
iuvo iuvare iuvi iūtum to help, please, delight

labellum -i, n (*diminutive form*) lip
lābēs -is, f spot, stain, blemish
labor -ōris, m hard work, toil
lac lactis, n milk
laedo laedere laesi laesum to hurt, strike, injure, offend
languidus -a -um faint, weak, feeble, inactive
lascīvia -ae, f playfulness, wantonness, licentiousness
lascīvus -a -um playful, wanton, licentious
lassus -a um tired, weary
lateo -ēre to lie hidden, be concealed
latus -eris, n side
laus laudis, f fame, glory
laxus -a -um loose, relaxed
lectus -i, m bed
lēna -ae, f procuress, madame (one who procures prostitutes for another's use)
lēnis -e gentle, soft, smooth
levis -e light, soft, gentle
lex lēgis, f law
licet licēre licūit it is allowed, one may
līnea -ae, f boundary line
lingua -ae, f tongue
liquidus -a -um flowing, liquid
līvor -ōris, m dark spot
loquor loqui locūtus sum to speak
lōrum -i, n pl reins; **lōra dare** to relax the reins
lūcus -i, m sacred grove / wood, wood

Vocabulary

lūmen -inis, n light, eye
lux lūcis, f light, day

macula -ae, f spot, blemish
magis more, to a greater extent
maior, maius greater, larger
male badly
manus -ūs, f hand
marītus -i, m husband
Mars Martis, m Mars (god of war)
Martigena -ae, m born of Mars
mēcum with me
memor -oris mindful, remembering
mens mentis, f mind
meretrix -īcis, f prostitute, whore
mēta -ae, f turning post
metuo -uere -ui -ūtum to fear
metus -ūs, m fear
Mīlanion -ōnis, m Milanion (husband of Atalanta)
mille a thousand
Minerva -ae, f Minerva (goddess of wisdom, science and creative arts)
minimus -a -um very small, smallest
minus less
mōbilis -e moving, moveable
mōbilitās -ātis, f mobility, movement
modestus -a -um moderate, restrained
modo only, just
modus -i, m manner, way
mora -ae, f delay, period of time
morior mori mortuus sum moritūrus to die
moror -ari to delay
mōs mōris, m custom, manner, practice
mōtus -ūs, m movement, motion
moveo movēre mōvi mōtum to move, set in motion
mūnus -eris, n office, duty, favour, gift

nascor nasci nātus sum to be born
necesse necessary (*indecl. adj.*)
nego -are to deny, refuse, say that not
nempe certainly, of course
Neptūnus -i, m Neptune (brother of Jupiter and god of the sea)
nēquitia -ae, f worthlessness, wantonness
nescioquis -quid someone, something
nescius -a -um ignorant, unaware
niger -gra -grum black, dark coloured
nīl = nihil nothing
nimium very much, too much
nītor nīti nīsus sum to strive, exert oneself
niveus -a -um white as snow
nix nivis, f snow
nōbilis -e famous, celebrated
nocturnus -a -um of the night, nocturnal
nondum not yet
nota -ae, f mark, sign
noto -are mark
nōtus -a -um known
nūper recently

obscēnus -a -um filthy, indecent, obscene
obsequium -i, n compliance, submission, indulgence
occlūdo -clūdere -clūsi -clūsum to close / shut up
ocellus -i, m eye (*diminutive form*)
oculus -i, m eye
ōdi ōdisse to hate, dislike
oppōno -pōnere -posui -positum to put opposite / before
opto -are to wish
opus -eris, n work, task
orbis -is, m circle
ōs ōris, n mouth
ovis -is, f sheep

pābulum -i, n food, fodder

paene nearly, almost

palam openly

pallium -i, n a light cloak (Greek in style)

palma -ae, f palm-branch (the token of victory)

parco parcere peperci parsum (+*dat*) to spare, keep oneself away from

pasco pascere pāvi pastum to feed, nourish, lead to pasture; *deponent* (+*abl*) – to feed on, graze

passus -a -um spread out

pateo -ēre to be open, stand open

patior pati passus sum to suffer, put up with, allow

pax pācis, f peace

pecco -are to make a mistake, err, sin, transgress

pectus -oris, n heart

pelagus -i, n the open sea

Pelops -opis, m Pelops (son of Tantalus, father of Atreus, grandfather of Agamemnon)

pendo pendere pependi pensum to hang down, dangle

Pēnelopē -ēs, f Penelope (the wife of Odysseus, who remained famously faithful to him during his long absence at Troy)

per (+*acc*) through, among, *in oaths:* by ...

perago -agere -ēgi -actum to go through, mention

perdo -dere -didi -ditum to destroy, ruin

perennis -e lasting, durable

pēs pedis, m foot

petulans -antis impudent, wanton, lascivious

Phoebē -ēs, f Pheobe (i.e. Diana, sister of Apollo, goddess of hunting)

Phoebus -i, m Apollo (god of prophecy)

pingo pingere pinxi pictum to paint, draw

pinna -ae, f feather, wing

placeo -ēre -ui -itum to please, be agreeable to

plāco -are to calm, reconcile, appease

plaudo plaudere plausi plausum to applaud, clap

plausus -ūs, m applause

Pollux -ūcis, m Pollux (a god renowned for his skill at boxing; twin brother of Castor)

pompa -ae, f procession

postis -is, m door-post, door
potens -entis powerful
potestās -ātis, f power (to do something), opportunity
praetor -ōris, m praetor (a senior Roman magistrate)
prātum -i, n meadow, meadow-grass
precor precari precatus sum to pray
premo premere pressi pressum to press hard / upon, squeeze
pretium -i, n price
prior prius former, previous
probrum -i, n abuse, reproach, grounds for reproach, disgrace
probus -a -um good, virtuous, excellent, honourable
procul far away, at a distance
procus -i, m suitor
profiteor -fiteri -fessus sum to acknowledge openly, confess
prōnus -a -um inclined towards, favourable
prostituo -stituere -stitui -stitūtum to prostitute, expose (to public shame)
prōtinus immediately
proximus -a -um nearest, very near
pudeo -ēre to cause shame
pudīcus -a -um chaste, virtuous
pudor -ōris, m sense of shame, decency
pugil -ilis, m boxer
pulvis eris, m dust
purpureus -a -um purple, dark red
puto -are to think, consider

quadriiugus -a -um in / with a team of four
quamvīs although
quia because
quīcumque quaecumque quodcumque whoever, whichever, whatever
quīdam quaedam quoddam a certain
Quirīs -ītis, m Roman citizen
Quirītes -um, m pl Quirites (another name for the citizens of Rome)
quisque quaeque quidque each, every
quisquis quaequae quidquid whoever, whichever, whatever

rāmus -i, m branch
rapio rapere rapui raptum to seize / tear away
ratus -a -um ratified, approved
recens -entis fresh, recent
recipio -cipere -cēpi -ceptum to take back, receive
recūso -are to object to, protest against, refuse
reddo -dere -didi -ditum to give back, give in return, give as one's due,
     pay up
refero referre rettuli relatum to bring back, restore, report
reluctor -ari to struggle against, resist
Remus -i Remus (twin brother to Romulus, and killed by him in quarrel
     over seniority at Rome's foundation)
reperio reperire repperi repertum to find, discover
resero -are to unbolt, open
revoco -are to recall, call back, regurgitate
rīdeo rīdēre rīsi rīsum to laugh, smile
rigidus -a -um stiff, unbending, inflexible, hard
Rōmulus -i Romulus (the founder and first king of Rome)
rostrum -i, n beak
rota -ae, f wheel
rūmino -are to chew the cud, chew over again
rūricola -ae, m country dweller
rusticus -a -um rustic, countrified, backward, provincial

sacer sacra sacrum sacred
saltem at least
sanguis -inis, m blood
sapio sapere sapīvi to be sensible, wise
satis enough
saxum -i, n rock
scīlicet evidently, certainly, of course
scio scire scīvi scītum to know, understand
secundus -a -um favourable
sēmen -inis, n seed
sequor sequi secūtus sum to follow, pursue
sera -ae, f door-bolt

sevērus -a -um severe, harsh, austere
sicco -are to make dry
signum -i, n sign
sine (+*abl*) without
singulus -a -um one at a time, individually
sinister -tra -trum left (hand side), wrong, perverse, unfavourable
sino sinere sīvi situm to allow
sinus -ūs, m curve, bend (*in pl*: arms, embrace, lap, folds of a toga)
somnus -i, m sleep
sono sonare sonūi sonitum to sound, make a noise
sordidus -a -um dirty, filthy, lowly
spargo spargere sparsi sparsum to scatter, sprinkle
spatiōsus -a -um ample, wide
spatium -i, n open space, distance, race course
spectāculum -i, n show, spectacle
sponda -ae, f bed-frame, bed
spūma -ae, f foam, froth
strīdeo strīdēre strīdi to make a loud noise, creak, hiss
stringo stringere strinxi strictum to draw tight together, to graze
studeo -ēre -ui (+*dat*) to be keen on, strive after
studiōsus -a -um keen on, devoted to
subeo -īre -ii -itum to come up upon, approach
submitto -mittere -mīsi -missum to let down, lower
subsum -esse -fui to be near, close to
succinctus -a -um having one's clothes tucked up in one's belt
summoveo -movēre -mōvi -mōtum to move away, drive off
supero -are to prevail, have the upper hand, overcome
supersum -esse -fui -futurus to remain, be left over
suspicor -ari to suspect, guess
sustineo -tinēre -tinui -tentum to hold up, support, to hold back / restrain

tabella -ae, f small writing tablet
tālis -e of such a kind, such
tantum only
taurus -i, m bull

tēcum with you
tego tegere texi tectum to cover
tempto -are to attempt, try to
tempus -oris, n time, occasion
tenax -ācis holding fast, gripping, obstinate
tendo tendere tetendi tentum to stretch out, extend
teneo tenēre tenui tentum to hold up, support, to hold back / restrain
tener -era -erum tender, soft, youthful
tenuis -e fine, thin
ter three times
tergum -i, n the back, body of an animal
testis -is, m/f witness
thalamus -i, m an inner room in a house, bedroom (most often a woman's bedroom)
timor -ōris, m fear
toga -ae, f toga
tollo tollere sustuli sublātum to lift up, raise
torreo torrēre torrui tostum to burn, scorch, dry up with heat
torus -i, m bed, mattress
totiens so often, so many times
tremo -ere -ui to tremble, quake
tueor tuēri tūitus sum to watch over, guard
tunc then
tunica -ae, f tunic
turbo -are to disturb, throw into disorder

ullus -a -um any
ūmidus -a -um wet, damp
unda -ae, f wave, water
undique from / on all sides
usque thoroughly, all the way
uterque utraque utrumque each (of two), both

vacca -ae, f cow
vacuus -a -um empty
validus -a -um strong, powerful

varius -a -um various, diverse
veho vehere vexi vectum to carry, convey; *passive* – to sail, ride, drive
vel or
vēnor -ari to hunt
ventus -i, m wind
Venus -eris, f Venus (goddess of love)
verber -eris, n whip
verbum -i, n word
verto vertere verti versum to turn
vērum -i, n truth, reality
vestis -is, f garment, piece of clothing
veto vetare vetui vetitum to forbid, prohibit
Victōria -ae, f Victory
videor vidēri vīsus sum to seem, appear
viduus -a -um deprived, destitute
vinclum -i, n bond, cord, chain
vīres -ium, f strength
virgo -inis, f maiden, virgin
viridis -e green
vitium -i, n fault, imperfection, crime
vīto -are to avoid
voluptās -ātis, f enjoyment, pleasure (especially sensual pleasure)
vōtum -i, n prayer, wish
vultus -ūs, m face, expression